Advance Praise for *Good White Racist?*

"Kerry Connelly is courageously helping to lead the charge to liberate white people from their own failed conception of goodness and, instead, inviting them to become true allies in the liberation of all God's people. In this book, good white people will find the truth. If they allow it, the truth shall set them free. Then we shall all be finally free."
—From the foreword by Michael W. Waters

"What Kerry has started is the hard work of 'white folk work' in a stunning and powerful volume that acknowledges the problem of white supremacy and its demonic effects on the American landscape and faith and her complicity in it. Always skeptical of white folks publishing books about the work I consider my life's calling, I walked into this book with the armor only a lifetime of oppression as a queer Black man can develop. What I was met with was a sincere partner in the struggle for my survival and someone who could speak into spaces I'll never be heard. This work is something to be read, shared, lived, and celebrated for that fact alone."
—Rev. Lenny Duncan, author of *Dear Church: A Love Letter from a Black Preacher to the Whitest Denomination in the U.S.*

"*Good White Racist?* offers a razor-sharp and readable analysis of the covert racism perpetrated by white people who mean well. Connelly tackles these topics in a way that encourages personal insight and accountability. Her frank observations (and occasional snark) make for a relatable book that left me cringing with recognition and motivated to change. It's an important read for all white people."
—Kristen Howerton, author of *Rage against the Minivan*

"No one wants to be called racist—or, worse, confess that we are—but the truth is we're all swimming in the toxic waters of America's cultural, systemic racism. Our choice is whether to ignore and deny it or to open our eyes to the ways we as white people (often unknowingly) perpetuate and benefit from racial injustice. For people of goodwill, the choice is clear, and Kerry Connelly offers a challenging yet accessible guide to recognizing our unconscious biases, our techniques of avoidance, and the myths we've believed about our history and ourselves."
—Jonathan Merritt, contributing writer for *The Atlantic* and author of *Learning to Speak God from Scratch*

"The work that needs to be done is white-on-white race talk. By that I mean, white folks talking to white folks about the ways white supremacy is internalized and therefore shows up in their social practice. Kerry endeavors to do just this, and I think we all should invest our time in this book!"
—Dr. Robyn Henderson-Espinoza, author of *Activist Theology*

"There are few things scarier than having to admit when we're wrong. Scarier yet is having to admit when those wrongs are racist thoughts and attitudes. But in *Good White Racist?*, Kerry Connelly faces that fear head on, confessing not only to her own racism but, in the process, opening the door to a desperately needed conversation about the latent racism that has permeated white American Christianity for generations. This book won't hold your hand and tell you everything will be alright. If anything, it will be quite painful to read, especially if you're a white guy like me who wants to think he doesn't have a racist bone in his body. But that's a good thing. Because repentance and transformation are painful, and white American Christianity has a lot to atone for whether we want to admit it or not."
—Zack Hunt, writer, speaker, and author of *Unraptured: How End Times Theology Gets It Wrong*

"Kerry Connelly masterfully challenges her white-identifying readers to reflect, repent, and then reimagine a new way to deconstruct the hierarchy that continually oppresses Black, indigenous people of color (BIPOC). I challenge those of us who carry unearned privilege because of our whiteness to read this book, put on our 'big kid underpants,' and help change the embedded systemic structures that are causing harm to our BIPOC siblings."
—Jonathan Williams, author of *She's My Dad: A Father's Transition and a Son's Redemption*, leader, and founder of Forefront Church in Brooklyn, New York

"This book is a necessary read for all white people. Seriously. All of us. *Good White Racist?* is provocative, eye-opening, offensive, and powerful. And it will humble even the most progressively aware white person. Connelly's approach is self-reflective, sharp-witted, and thoughtfully researched. I needed this book. You do too."
—Matthew Paul Turner, author of *When God Made the World and When I Pray for You*

Good White Racist?

Good White Racist?

Confronting Your Role in Racial Injustice

KERRY CONNELLY

WESTMINSTER
JOHN KNOX PRESS
LOUISVILLE • KENTUCKY

First edition
Published by Westminster John Knox Press
Louisville, Kentucky

20 21 22 23 24 25 26 27 28 29—10 9 8 7 6 5 4 3 2

Book design by Sharon Adams
Cover design by Mark Abrams

Library of Congress Cataloging-in-Publication Data

Names: Connelly, Kerry, author.
Title: Good white racist? : confronting your role in racial injustice / Kerry Connelly.
Description: First edition. | Louisville, Kentucky : Westminster John Knox Press, 2020. |
Summary: "When it comes to race, most White Americans are obsessed with two things: defending our own inherent goodness and maintaining our own comfort levels. Too often, this means white people assume that to be racist, one has to be openly hateful and willfully discriminatory-you know, a bad person. And we know we're good, Christian people, right? But you don't have to be wearing a white hood or shouting racial epithets to be complicit in America's racist history and its ongoing systemic inequality. In Good White Racist?, Kerry Connelly exposes the ways white people participate in, benefit from, and unknowingly perpetuate racism-despite their best "good person" intentions. Good White Racist? unpacks the systems that maintain the status quo, keep white people comfortable and complicit, and perpetuate racism in the United States and elsewhere. Combining scholarly research with her trademark New Jersey snark, Connelly shows us that even though it may not be our fault or choice to participate in a racist system, we all do, and it's our responsibility to do something about it"—Provided by publisher.
Identifiers: LCCN 2019057102 (print) | LCCN 2019057103 (ebook) | ISBN 9780664265748 (paperback) | ISBN 9781611649901 (ebook)
Subjects: LCSH: Racism—Religious aspects—Christianity. | Racism—United States. | Race discrimination—Religious aspects—Christianity. | Race discrimination—United States. | Whites—Race identity. | United States—Race relations.
Classification: LCC BT734.2 .C66 2020 (print) | LCC BT734.2 (ebook) | DDC 277.308/3089—dc23
LC record available at https://lccn.loc.gov/2019057102
LC ebook record available at https://lccn.loc.gov/2019057103

Contents

Foreword   vii

Author's Note   xi

Acknowledgments   xiii

Introduction   1

1. The Good Nation of America   9
   (Or, *We're Good, but Not as Good as We Think*)

2. The White Empire   25
   (Or, *You're Not White—You Just Think You Are*)

3. Gaslit and Ghosted   37
   (Or, *They're Not Protesting the Flag—and You Know It*)

4. The Power of Language   59
   (Or, *Are You Freaking Kidding Me? No, You Can't Use the N-Word*)

5. The Mis-education of America   71
   (Or, *Everything You Know about Being a Good White Racist You Probably Learned in Kindergarten*)

6. Justifying Ourselves   85
   (Or, *"But Black People Owned Slaves!"*)

7. White People's Posse   101
   (Or, *You Just* Think *You Need to Call the Police*)

8. Unequal Justice   111
   (Or, *Liberty and Justice for All White People
   and White People Only*)

9. The Consumption of Bodies   119
   (Or, *"Step Away from the Hair"*)

10. Shiny Happy People   131
    (Or, *When Good White Racists Go to Church*)

11. In Full Color   143
    (Or, *Where We Go from Here*)

    Notes   163

Foreword

The names of C. C. J. Carpenter, Joseph A. Durick, Milton L. Grafman, Paul Hardin, Nolan B. Harmon, George M. Murray, Edward V. Ramage, and Earl Stallings are not readily known by most of the American populace. But together, these men left an indelible mark on the American Civil Rights Movement. In Birmingham, Alabama, in 1963, each of these men would have considered themselves among the ranks of the good white people of the nation, especially with regard to race.

They were not.

These clergymen were white moderates. Compared to some other white people, they may have even fancied themselves progressives. Birmingham led the nation in unsolved bombings, and *they* were not personally bombing anyone. Still, they could not stomach what they deemed to be lawlessness in the streets.

Earlier that year, Fred Shuttlesworth, once called "the most courageous civil rights fighter in the South" by none other than Martin Luther King, Jr., invited Dr. King and the Southern Christian Leadership Conference to Birmingham to support desegregation efforts in the city. On Good Friday, April 12, 1963, the same day Dr. King was arrested in Birmingham, these "good" white clergymen offered a scathing rebuke of Dr. King and his efforts in an open letter they titled "A Call for Unity." They wrote, "we are now confronted by a series of demonstrations by some of our Negro citizens, directed and led in part by outsiders. We recognize the natural impatience of people who feel that their hopes are slow in being realized. But we are convinced that these demonstrations are unwise and untimely."[1]

There is a certain level of gall that one must possess to seek to set the timetable and parameters by which a people should achieve their liberation, and these clergymen possessed it in abundance.

Such is the gall of whiteness.

Such is the gall of white privilege.

Such is an accomplice of white supremacy.

In response to their letter, Dr. King offered what can only be described as the greatest treatise on nonviolent direct action penned in the twentieth century. He wrote,

> You deplore the demonstrations taking place in Birmingham. But your statement, I am sorry to say, fails to express a similar concern for the conditions that brought about the demonstrations. I am sure that none of you would want to rest content with the superficial kind of social analysis that deals merely with effects and does not grapple with underlying causes. It is unfortunate that demonstrations are taking place in Birmingham, but it is even more unfortunate that the city's white power structure left the Negro community with no alternative.[2]

Then Dr. King brought things into clearer view, removing from these clergymen any semblance of progression or allyship. He wrote,

> I must confess that over the past few years I have been gravely disappointed with the white moderate. I have almost reached the regrettable conclusion that the Negro's great stumbling block in his stride toward freedom is not the White Citizen's Counciler or the Ku Klux Klanner, but the white moderate, who is more devoted to "order" than to justice; who prefers a negative peace which is the absence of tension to a positive peace which is the presence of justice;

who constantly says: "I agree with you in the goal you seek, but I cannot agree with your methods of direct action"; who paternalistically believes he can set the timetable for another man's freedom; who lives by a mythical concept of time and who constantly advises the Negro to wait for a "more convenient season." Shallow understanding from people of good will is more frustrating than absolute misunderstanding from people of ill will.[3]

It is the unfortunate continuation of this misguided and dangerous sense of privilege and pseudo-supremacy that Kerry Connelly masterfully confronts in this book. Just like in 1963, there are many "good" white people who readily denounce racist words and racial violence. They may even openly express their concerns regarding the near-constant slaughter of unarmed Black men, women, boys, and girls at the hands of police. However, these same "good" white people denounce present-day nonviolent direct-action protests, including the kneeling of American athletes during the National Anthem, as untimely, unwise, and unpatriotic. Some "good" white people believe it their duty to correct proclamations that "Black lives matter!" with the proclamation that "all lives matter!"

These "good" white people criticize Black and Brown people for low voter turnout in national and local elections yet remain eerily silent on issues of voter intimidation, voter disenfranchisement, the gutting of voter protections in the highest court in the land, the gerrymandering of Black and Brown communities, and the failure of all political parties to adequately address policy issues that would transform their lived-in realities. They readily employ such words as "colorblind" to describe themselves and their hopes for our racial future, and they are quick to quote Dr. King about the importance of love and unity. However, they consistently fail to speak about racial equity, and they fail to uplift Dr. King's call for reparations, a guaranteed income for all Americans, and a congressional act for the disenfranchised. In intimate settings, they employ microaggressions, touch and talk about Black women's hair without invitation, and think it is a compliment to call a Black person "articulate" to their face.

Indeed, "shallow understanding from people of good will is more frustrating than absolute misunderstanding from people of ill will." This is frequently the peril of "good" white people. Oft times, they are certain that they are helping when they are only helping to preserve a death-dealing status quo. Even when welcoming persons of other racial and ethnic backgrounds into certain spaces, whiteness is often uplifted as normative, and assimilation is often the unspoken goal.

During these still troubled days in America, days where "good" white people frequently call the police on Black people for such mundane activities as meeting in a coffee shop or cutting grass, where the legacy of redlining and racial wealth disparities remain, where thousands of Black and Brown people remain incarcerated for activities presently earning "good" white people outrageous profits, Kerry Connelly is courageously helping to lead the charge to liberate white people from their own failed conception of goodness and, instead, inviting them to become true allies in the liberation of all God's people.

In this book, "good" white people will find the truth.

If they allow it, the truth shall set them free.

Then we shall all be finally free.

Michael W. Waters
Dallas, Texas

Author's Note

I enter this work with humility (despite any snark you may encounter in the coming pages), and I know there are many BIPOC (Black, indigenous people of color) who are doing this work and have been for decades. I enter this work holding a firm belief that white people must be doing antiracist work first and foremost within our own psyches and emotional landscapes. Only then can we hope to lead other white people in the work of antiracism, and ultimately submit to the leadership of the BIPOC community. My goal is to come alongside the amazing leaders who are already doing this work from the perspective of living in historically oppressed bodies; it is not my intention to displace or usurp those invaluable voices. I dance on the thin line of wanting to own and carry the emotional labor that should have belonged to white people this whole time while simultaneously respecting and honoring the beautiful, laborious work already done by the BIPOC community. I am certainly not the first white person to dance here, but there are nowhere near enough of us at this party.

To my white friends: Fair warning—this is going to be hard. It's going to get real, and you're going to be uncomfortable. I know well the discomfort you're about to encounter, and stronger souls than you have declined the experience. So find something to grab onto, because I'm not mincing words here. But I promise you that if you're truly the good person you think you are and know you want to be, it will be worth it.

The time is urgent: people are dying.

To readers in the BIPOC community: Beautiful soul, thank you for reading even this far. This book is by a white person for white people, and you do not owe us your participation in this dialogue. You've done enough, borne enough of this weight. It's our turn now. That said, I'm not trying to be your hero and I do not want to put words into your mouths. I do not speak for people of color, nor do I wish to even remotely play the role of "white savior." I think we all have our redemptive work to do in the world—the wrong thing we are to try to make right—even if we do it poorly and make a mess of things. This speaking to white people about whiteness and racism is simply the work that has my name on it.

That said, if I say anything that perpetuates harm, and you feel like it is worth your energy, please call me on it. Send me an email or write a review. I do care to learn. If you see something in these pages and care to take issue with it, I welcome your words. Thank you for reading. And most of all, I ask forgiveness, if you have any left to give.

Acknowledgments

Everything I know about race and whiteness I have learned from people of color who are doing the hard labor of racial justice work. They deserve top billing for the work they do in the world. Some of them I have had the pleasure of learning from personally and others only from their public work, but my own racial awakening and this work would never have happened without them.

I have learned from Ruby Sales, Jacqueline J. Lewis, Monica Coleman, Carlton Waterhouse, David Moore, Nadine Smith, and Mark Charles, and they have opened my theological and racial awareness exponentially. Black writers whose work has fed my soul include Austin Channing-Brown, James Baldwin, Zora Neale Hurston, Martin Luther King Jr., Ta-Nehisi Coates, Toni Morrison, Alice Walker, Maya Angelou, and Kwame Alexander. Robyn Henderson-Espinoza was gracious to allow me to share the story of the day they schooled me on Twitter. Kathy Khang is the person who first helped me see the concept of white goodness as a barrier to racial awakening. To these incredible teachers, I say thank you.

Nate Nakao and H. Jacquim Ross generously shared their experiences with me and allowed them to be retold in this book.

A number of people offered their guidance and insight to this project throughout the writing process. Cleve Tinsley of Project Curate reviewed parts of the manuscript and made it better. And

I am forever indebted to Lisa Boeving-Learned, a friend who has generously offered her professional insight into the criminal justice system. Scott Seay assisted with research, and Alan Rhoda of the library at Christian Theological Seminary was invaluable in providing resources.

Two very special people took on the painful process of reading first drafts. Samantha Kline, your loving wisdom guided this project from day one, and I am eternally grateful not just for that effort but for your friendship as well. I can't wait to return the favor. Benjamin J. Tapper, you have been a guardian angel standing sentry over this project, and it's been an honor to incorporate your insights into the work. Thank you for keeping me real. Your friendship is priceless to me. I love you both.

Aisha Irvis and Nicole Mendolera keep me laughing and relatively sane every day of my life. For fro-yo and long walks in the park, my thanks and love.

Jessica Miller Kelley made this work infinitely better, and I would not be willing to put it out into the world without her expert eye overseeing its construction. Infinite thanks to you and the team at Westminster John Knox Press.

Of course, my husband, Michael—who holds down the fort, makes sure our family is all fed, watered, and wearing clean clothes when I am in the throes of procrastination—deserves more credit than I can ever offer. I love you, and I am so lucky to ride this ride with you.

And to my children, Delaney and Evan, who are always careful not to disturb me when I'm writing, thank you for being amazing children who are already asking the question, "Wait, is this racist?" You give me hope that a better world might actually be possible. I love you.

Introduction

Hi. I'm Kerry, and I'm a racist. (This is where you're supposed to say, "Hi, Kerry.")

But I want you to know that I'm a *good* racist. I don't wear my white sheet over my smiling face. Instead, it's on the inside, where it wraps my heart in fear I desperately wish wasn't there. It's tangled up in my brain, where thoughts flash by at lightning speed before I even have the time to examine them. And it's the sweet satin feel of my privileged skin that lets me slide easily through my every day. Because the truth is, as much as I'd like it not to be true, it's totally possible that I'm a really good person, and a really big racist all at the same time.

Before we all get our knickers in a twist, as my grandmother used to say, let me be clear that this is not a "There are good people on all sides" kind of idea. First of all, I'm not talking about neo-Nazis or the KKK. These are people who have made racist ideology their center of being, a prospect that I find disturbing and disgusting. They are not who I am talking about when I talk about good white racists. Rather, I'm referring to the majority of white people who intellectually believe that racism is evil, that being "color-blind" is good, and who get so uncomfortable talking about race that they will tell racial activists to shut up about it because "it's just making it worse." I'm talking about progressives like me who, in our desire to help tend instead to do more

1

harm, who talk a great game on the one hand while maintaining the racist status quo on the other. I'm talking about white people like some of my family members who wouldn't hesitate to jump in the water to save a Black person who was drowning but who also, deep down inside—where they might not even realize it's there—hold the belief that there is something inherently defective about that Black body that made it less able to swim and be completely oblivious to the fact that white America limited Black people's access to swimming pools and beaches for generations.

I am one of these good white racists. Though I never had specific thoughts about racialized swimming abilities, I confess there was a time when I held a belief that there was an inherent difference between me and people of color. I didn't know where it came from; it was just there, kind of like my hair or my name. I never questioned its existence—and worse, I never noticed how it operated in my psyche or how it impacted my view of the world.

In fact, for most of my life, I preferred not to talk about race. It's so . . . *uncomfortable.* And like I said, I'm a *good* racist. The kind who really loves Martin Luther King Jr.'s *I Have a Dream* speech, until it comes time to actually do something to manifest said dream. The kind who loves to watch movies about white heroes saving poor Black people from poverty and lives of crime (a stereotype and a fallacy that perpetuates white supremacy). The kind who likes to call herself an *ally,* until my allyship requires action and/or makes me uncomfortable.

I share all those memes about social justice, after all. I voted for Obama. I curse like a truck driver, but I would *never* use the "N" word. And my feelings got *really* hurt when Uncle Bob made that comment about me being a snowflake.

I mean, I'm practically a social justice *warrior.*

You might be like me. And, like me, you might be awakening to the fact that you're all tangled up in your own internal white sheets, and it might be making you super squirmy. Or maybe you're saying, "What sheets? Where? I don't have any sheets. I'm a good person, remember?" Maybe you're sitting in church on Sunday morning, enjoying the choir's performance of a gospel song and hearing how there are no different ethnicities or genders, no "slave or free" because we're all "one in Christ Jesus" (Gal. 3:28). Then you're going home to watch the game and wondering if maybe the Take a Knee Movement couldn't find a more convenient, more *patriotic* way to protest, or whatever.[1] Maybe you're all about being politically correct, but deep down you don't *really* think racism is that big of a deal. So someone told a racist joke. So what? It's not like it's a hate crime—or actual slavery. People need to relax and stop being so serious all the time. And besides, Oprah is like, a trillionaire or something, so obviously Black people are just fine.

Listen—I get you. You don't want to be racist, and the fact that I'm even suggesting you might be has you all bunched up inside the way sand gets twisted up in your bathing suit at the beach. I know that sometimes you probably think, *Seriously, can't we just get over this race thing already?* It's all pretty exhausting, and you have no idea what to say or do to make it better anyway, so you'd really rather just go ahead and get your yoga on and meditate it all away in your Lululemons (or, if you're like me, your Lululemon knockoffs, because who can afford that shit?).

If you're a white guy, it's probably even harder for you, because you're really tired of being held up as the epitome of all evil in America by progressives like me. I get it. That probably sucks a lot, especially when you're just trying to get by, and maybe enjoy life a little bit. After all, you've worked hard for what you've got. And besides, we live in the land of opportunity, where everyone has a fair shot and there is liberty and justice for all. We just have to go out and grab that golden ring, and make our way in the world.

I know these arguments well. I've not only been subjected to them by countless people who disagree with me, but I've actually used them myself in what seems like a previous lifetime—a time when I was so afraid someone would think I wasn't good that I was afraid to say the word "Black" in front of a Black person. As in, "Hey, can you hand me that sweater? No, not that one. The *black* one." I'd rather walk around in a hot pink and lime green sweater than say "Black" in front of a Black person, lest they think I meant something by it and say that I was racist.

And this is partly because the few times I *did* make an attempt at acknowledging race, I did it poorly and suffered the indignant response from the people of color in front of whom I'd just made an ass out of myself. As a result, I shied away from acknowledging this huge, seemingly cavernous difference between us. I decided to pretend skin color didn't exist. I proudly considered myself color-blind, determined to see anything and everything but the full, complete identity of the people in the room—myself included. The hardest identity for me to see and acknowledge was the one that has been rendered the most invisible to me by society: my own whiteness.

I was, back then, *very* good at being a good white racist—simultaneously both racially unconscious and hyperaware, terrified of saying the wrong thing and yet blissfully unaware of the myriad ways my privilege, my power, and my whiteness as a white woman were at play in every interaction I had with people of color. As a follower of Jesus who attended diverse churches, I believed I had already arrived at the shores of a postracial society; I had Black friends, so obviously, everything was fine. My whiteness was the elephant in the room, the unspoken truth that wielded power in the relationship whether I wanted it to or not.

I think there are tons of white people like me—people with good intentions who are not only completely unaware of the way their own power operates in the world but who also like it that way. Because this is true, it is *our* job—white people, not anyone else's—to acknowledge this power dynamic and then dismantle it, making space for the power of others to emerge.

To do this, we need to notice the systems, institutions, and structures that we all navigate every day—from government, to our language, to our cultural practices and gender roles, to work environments, religious practices, family dynamics, and our criminal justice system—because they all work to support and perpetuate this imbalance of power. By participating in these systems without ever questioning or challenging them, we support it too.

The fact that white people can go through life without ever having to do any really uncomfortable thinking about race is itself a privilege that people of color simply don't have. I've heard white people say they don't feel "educated or well-equipped enough" to talk about race in any but the most intimate circles. This too is a privileged cop-out. My guess is that most people of color aren't born learning how to navigate the racial biases they encounter every day. There's no "how to be Black and Brown" school. They figure it out as they go as a matter of survival. They teach the inexplicable to their children around the dinner table and on the way to driver education classes and during bath time. To say you are not educated or well equipped or passionate enough to talk about race is really just about you wanting to stay safe and comfortable.

Doing the work of dismantling racism is boundary walking at its finest. It's a high-wire act with no net. It's crossing borders and saying the wrong thing and learning from it when you do. It's being willing to be uncomfortable; it's being willing to say you're sorry; and for the love of all that is good and holy, it's being willing to do your own damn work. And for the record, you don't need to accost the next person of color you see and dive into a deep heart-to-heart about your white goodness and all those racists *out there*.

That is *not* doing the work.

Doing the work is picking up your own burden, doing the research, reading the work of the multitude of voices out there that are different from yours. It's learning from people of color, listening to their stories—and when they tell you how they feel, it's resisting the urge to explain to them why they should feel differently. It's studying how racism (and other "isms") works and committing to doing things differently in your own corner of the world. Doing the work is dismantling all the usual justifications that populate the gotcha memes on Facebook and maybe even your own brain cells. It's being able to look at these issues through the lens of our own whiteness, because it is within whiteness that the problem lies. Hell, it's being able to recognize that you even have a lens to begin with, and understanding that this lens colors the way you see—or don't see—everything.

I'm not saying that we're not good people, you and me. I'm just asking for us to *act* like the good people we are. I'm asking that we all #NoticeTheSystem, that we self-identify as

#GoodWhiteRacists and call that shit out. And yes, I'm saying hashtag the hell out of it. When we see it, name it. It's the first daring, brave act of being truly antiracist in which you and I can participate. Because if even the first tiny step is all of us finally acknowledging that, Houston, we have a problem, I'd be happy. And since you're a good person and all, I know you want to be antiracist.

Right?

I also know this isn't easy. God knows it's not easy for me every time I discover another racist thought floating around my head or realize another way I'm complicit in the system. I know that I've probably already made you a little uncomfortable, if not outright pissed off. That's okay. Let's just sit with that for a hot second. Because honestly, our discomfort is not the problem. It's our absolute refusal to roll around in that discomfort that's the problem. It's the fact that we'd rather run from the room screaming, "I'm good! I'm good! I swear to God I'm good!" than actually sit and practice a tiny little bit of honest self-reflection.

Until we can take a good, hard look at who we are as white people, how we operate in the world, and what the systems are that maintain the status quo, race relations in America will not improve. Now, some of you may think that's totally fine. Some of you might be totally cool with that, because as of right now, you can't see any good reason to switch things up. But I'm saying if you want to be good, that attitude just ain't gonna fly.

Your neighbors—people of color—are practically drowning in our toxic whiteness. If you're a good person, when you see someone drowning, not only will you jump in to pull them out, but once you do, you'll also do the good hard work of building a safety fence around the pool they fell into in the first place—just like any good American hero would. You can't be a good person and ignore your drowning neighbor. You can't be a good person and let a dangerous situation continue when it threatens to consume your community.

What you can do, however, is *pretend* to be a good person. You can act like you don't hear the cries for help while you sit there on your deck with your little pink drink with the umbrella or your nice cold beer, determined to keep your eyes on the beautiful horizon, your line of sight hovering just over the pool where your neighbor is sputtering, trying desperately to tread water. You can pretend you don't hear, don't see, don't know. But that doesn't make you good.

In fact, that makes you pretty evil.

You know it, and I know it. So let's stop pretending, shall we? Let's agree, one way or the other. You can go ahead and put this book down now, keep your eyes on the horizon, your ears plugged tight, and your head held in the pride of your false goodness, your own inherent evil that shines so bright it makes you blind. Or you can be willing to wade into these deep, disturbing waters with me, even if it's cold and frightening and we're both really scared of what we're going to find.

Though I have studied this topic like crazy, I confess that I am still learning. In fact, I'm pretty sure it will be a lifelong project. I have had countless conversations about this topic in which I said stupid things, and I have read a lot about it (though still not enough). I have talked about this on the *White on White* podcast, and I have written about it on the *Jerseygirl, Jesus* blog (and suffered the trolls for it too). I have listened to people of color, I have hated my own self and cried my white tears and carried the burden of my own white, useless guilt, and now I can boldly and loudly tell you a secret: I am a good white racist.

And I am in recovery.

Chapter One

The Good Nation of America

(Or, *We're Good, but Not as Good as We Think*)

The books always smelled a little funny; even the dust that perpetually covered them seemed old and wise. I would flip through the pages and stare at hollowed-out eyes, protruding rib cages, and piles of shoes and eyeglasses. I would gaze into the ancient and wizened eyes of the American soldiers, shell-shocked and dazed, helmet straps loosened and hanging down by their chins. Faces dirtied by war, they appeared haunted by their witness of the purest evil. They were the unlucky few, the reluctant heroes, the ones who won the war and freed the Jews from the terrors of the Holocaust, from the horrors of Dachau and Mauthausen.

These Americans—they were *good*.

My father's old books proved it. There it was, captured in strangely faded pictures on pages that smelled a little funny and held the dust of the ages, and told in the stories of how the Americans swooped in to save the Jews, and the day.[1]

It's practically biblical, right?

The images of these American soldiers who freed the Holocaust survivors—happy, youthful couples dancing in the streets of New York, where joyful sailor boys kissed their lady folk in Times Square in celebration of a well-won victory[2] are embedded in our collective subconscious as a country. Americans are the heroes—the good guys, the proverbial knights in shining armor. We dance in the street while everyone else deals with the cold, harsh reality of what happens when people lose touch with their human side. We get to be shiny-toothed and gleaming. We get to be bright-eyed and optimistic, safe in the land of plenty. And all is as it should be.

Or is it?

It's almost as though we could follow a shiny, gleaming timeline that traces our own goodness. It could start with those first—well, let's call them *settlers* for now—the idealistic underdogs desperate for religious freedom and committed to creating freedom and justice for all (or at least, all white, land-owning men) while they forged a new territory with uncompromised ruggedness and neophyte American grit. I mean, I can practically feel the prairie dust under my fingernails. Fast-forward through the Civil War, and you'll see where America finally came to its moral senses, freed the slaves, and allegedly restored justice, the whole slavery thing being just an unfortunate blip on our otherwise spotless record. We can speed through the idealized suburbia and white-toothed, lobotomized commercials of the midcentury, flash through the uncomfortable discord of the 1960s, and head right to the fall of evil communism, to that day our movie-star president exclaimed, "Mr. Gorbachev, take down that wall!" and the fear of a *Red Dawn* was mitigated.

This has always been our collective identity as Americans. We are good, and our enemy is evil. To suggest otherwise is a sort of national heresy the likes of which can get you banned from any sports bar worth its salt. This is the history we teach in our schools, where kindergarteners celebrate that big ole party where the "Pilgrims and Indians" sat down together for a big turkey dinner. We maybe chastise Christopher Columbus for his shrewdness—but just a little—in the way he swindled the tribal chiefs out of their land for some pretty beads (but really, those silly, naive Indians should have known those beads were worthless, *chuckle, chuckle*). We don't mention the blankets laced with smallpox or the Trail of Tears. These things remain in the educational netherworld, truths to be discovered with the breaking of our own identities as we grow into our personhood as adults. For so many of us educated in the twentieth century—and perhaps even now—this is like discovering that Santa Claus isn't real, that our parents are human, that teachers have first names.

We hide from our own shadow side, unable to hold the paradox that as generally good people, we can do incredibly bad things. The truth is that if you look at the body of our work as a nation— the whole history, and not just the bits we like—there are two things that are true: First, America is gleaming. We are inherently idealistic, a beautiful experiment in human imagination and potential. Second, we are evil. We are a gluttonous machine of turning gears that mangle the souls of men, women, and children alike. And each one of us—every single one of us—is a participant in this absurdity.

What's a Good White Racist, Anyway?

Before we go any further, it might be helpful to dive a little deeper into how I'm using certain words, because I know that these words tend to be intense and to elicit strong reactions in many of us. Let's start with the big one: What is a good white racist, anyway?

Good

Americans have a sanitized version of goodness that often leaves little room for complexity or nuance. Our Sunday schools teach us that goodness is secured if we don't drink, smoke, or have sex, that our righteousness is guaranteed with a simple prayer of salvation. We were raised on a snack food of "good guys versus bad guys," with superheroes to save the day and villains with clearly defined low moral standards. Goodness doesn't come in layers in the American psyche; you either are, or you aren't— and once you aren't, you aren't forever. Good people, however, toe the line. They are nice and never disruptive, and they value peace and comfort and the status quo. Good people never make other people uncomfortable with their words. In fact, good people are fluent in the lexicon of niceness, where, for sure, no one ever mentions whiteness.

White

And whiteness? That's an interesting concept. We'll do a deep dive into the constructed identity that is whiteness in chapter 2, but it's important to understand from the get-go that whiteness is a social construct, not a biological one. Should you happen to have been born into a body that has paler skin, you have been automatically granted certain benefits and privileges that people with more melanin simply don't have. This is true even when you struggle to find a job or pay your bills or have to go to court or fail math class. White privilege means that even though your life may not be easy, the color of your skin does not provide additional obstacles to your success.

Because privilege is often invisible to those who have it, here's a handy list of some of the ways white privilege may operate—in society, and yes, in your life too. Keep in mind that intersectionality is also at play here. That means that your gender or sexual identity, your class, and your physical ability and embodiment may also interact with your racial identity to impact the way these privileges operate in your life.

Economic privilege is the ability to build generational wealth and to easily access the basic requirements of life: food, housing, clothing, and so forth, as well as luxuries such as private transportation, rest from labor, and decent health care.

Spatial privilege is the ability to move through space safely, without fear of violence perpetrated on your body by individuals or the state.

Educational privilege is the ability to feel certain that public education will meet your needs and not prohibit you from obtaining a quality education through educational geographical gerrymandering, instructor or administrative bias, or the school-to-prison pipeline. It is the ability to know that any disabilities or struggles you have in school will receive medical or curative interventions rather than criminal or punitive interventions.

Intellectual privilege is the ability to be recognized for your intellectual accomplishments and not erased from the public narrative. In school and in the workplace, your intellect is never questioned. Additionally, recognition for your accomplishments is not relegated to a single month of the year or a special table in the back for "white authors." Rather, your ideas are celebrated for their own right, alongside any other ideas of equal import.

Historical privilege is the ability to see members of your race accurately represented in history books and given credit for their contributions to society. The impact of social policies on your racial, ethnic, or gender group is portrayed appropriately. Your cultural practices throughout history are not diminished, considered "primitive" or less advanced.

Generational privilege is the ability to search for your roots and actually find them. It is the ability to know who your ancestors were.

Bodily privilege is the ability to move through society free from the judgment that your body's natural state does not meet a certain standard, and from people claiming some sort of ownership and the right to touch you.

As white people, once we understand the different types of privilege we enjoy, we can fight for the right to these privileges for others.

People—especially people with power—will think differently about you than they will people of color. As a result, they will go easier on you, offer you assistance rather than police your body, and be more likely to give you the benefit of the doubt when you mess up. In other words, people who have been assigned a white identity by society are often also presumed to be good and have to work really hard at proving otherwise. Meanwhile, good people of color are presumed automatically to be bad, often while they're just moving through the world, just trying to exist. That reality is not merely the result of the prejudiced actions of *some* white people. Rather, it is evidence of a pervasive, all-encompassing culture of systemic racism.

Racist

Because I know the R-word freaks everybody out, let's go about defining it too, because I mean something very specific when I use it. *Racism* refers to a system of hierarchy based on the belief that one race is superior to all others. Most often, and as is definitely the case in the United States, this manifests as both a collective social more and an individual belief. When combined with power—which is usually economic but can manifest in other ways—it becomes institutionalized.

Institutionalized racism is the way that belief becomes ingrained and reinforced in societal organizations, such as government, education, the judicial system, economics, and media (just to name a few).

Individual racism is a set of personal conscious or unconscious beliefs that assume one race is superior to all others. It is important to note that individual racism can be held by both the dominant and the oppressed person, but only in relation to the oppressed person. In other words, in the United States, where whiteness is held as the highest rank on the hierarchical system, *white people cannot be victims of racism.* So-called reverse racism is just not a thing, people. However, people of color may hold internalized racist views about their own race, and they may hold hierarchically racist beliefs about members of other groups (i.e., prejudice).

Systemic racism is the ways in which these types of racism work together to directly impact BIPOC on a large scale and privilege whites in the United States.

These qualities converge to create good white racists. First, good white racists are people who have been assigned the racial identity of whiteness. Second, good white racists are people who benefit from that assignment in a social system that privileges whiteness. Third, good white racists are generally nice people who intellectually do not approve of racist behaviors but who practice them anyway. Fourth, good white racists are—for a time, at least—unaware of the ways they benefit from and perpetuate racist systems that privilege them. Finally, good white racists generally respond with defensiveness when they are confronted with their participation in racist systems, because they are more concerned (possibly obsessed) with two things: their own comfort and their own inherent goodness.

The First Time I Was White

I can't say for sure that I didn't already know that strange, invisible lines divided us. I can't say for sure that I wasn't already feeling that awkward, invisible *thing*, unspoken and insidious, that laid a weight on my back that I could not name and that created an odd disharmony between me and the Black people I met. And disharmony is, indeed, the right word. Whatever this thing was, it kept us from falling into a beautiful, easy polyphony together, from bringing the different notes of our beauty together in a gorgeous symphony or a simple fugue. We were, together, disharmonious. And I had no idea why, nor did I have language to describe it.

I do a little digging in the coffers of memory, and a free-flowing stream of images begins to percolate. It's like old movies, or the faded pictures I found in an old box in my mother's basement. The mind pictures are slightly yellowed with the burnt mustard shades so common to the time, but for me, this can't conceal the whiteness that inserted itself into my psyche that day. There I am, probably no older than seven or eight, and my mother has agreed to babysit a young boy whose mother she had met in church. I was thrilled—a playmate for my lonely soul! My mother was the neighborhood extrovert, willing to talk to everyone, friendly and ready to shine a smile to everyone with equal exuberance. My mom never thought twice about babysitting the child, and that was part of the problem.

No. Let me not do that. My mother *should* have babysat the boy. She should not have had to think twice about babysitting the boy. My mother was not the problem—not entirely, anyway. The big problem was our next-door neighbor Rudy. And he was a problem because the little boy was Black.

Widowed for as long as I can remember, Rudy was a foul-mouthed, grumpy old man who would sit outside on his front steps in the summer months, smoking and occasionally yelling gruff instructions at the neighborhood kids, wearing only green work pants and a T-shirt stained yellow with sweat and tobacco. He was loud and a little scary, but generally he left us alone. Every once in a while, he would even offer me candy, but never without my mother there. Rudy was just as much a fixture of my summer days as the tall oak tree that stood sentry over my house and the green grass under my feet. Rudy was part of the neighborhood.

But something happened when Rudy saw that little boy, whom I only met that one time and whose name I don't remember. Rudy's voice got gruffer than normal. He said words I don't remember now and didn't understand then. And my mom said we couldn't play outside anymore that day.

Later, when the boy's mother came to get him, my mom sheepishly told her that she should no longer babysit him. She apologized profusely and explained it was nothing to do with the child, but that Rudy was to blame. She would hate for the boy to hear the disgusting words that Rudy would call him. She was happy to babysit but thought that the mother should know what she'd be exposing her son to. The young, beautiful mother looked sad and uncomfortable, thanked my mother, and never came back.

I remember feeling sad and awkward too. But I also felt something else: anger. Why would my mom not tell Rudy to shut up? Why did Rudy get to ruin everything? I did not fully understand everything that had happened, but I did understand that whatever it was, it was very, very bad, and that somehow my mother, by not standing up to Rudy, was complicit. And so was I.

That was a day of indoctrination for me, but it wasn't the first and was certainly not the only. Though I didn't know it at the time, I was surrounded by messages that taught me narratives about people of color and taught me to ignore my own whiteness. These stories normalized my identity, made it the center of the universe—the sea we all swim in, the air we breathe. This day taught me that grumpy old white men get to call the shots, that when confronted with racial injustice, mothers, both Black and white, and children, especially Black ones, don't get to matter. This day taught me that we don't fight these grumpy old white men—that they just get their way because they just get their way. Later, when I tried to ask my mom about it, she didn't need to whisper the word *Black* when she tried to help me understand. I already knew it was somehow a word that mattered, a word that needed to be whispered because it held some sort of magic power to make people incredibly uncomfortable.

The one word she never said at all, though, was *white*.

No one ever mentioned all the whiteness that was going on there. Everything was all about the Blackness. But the Blackness was simply being. It was whiteness that was the agitator, that got all uncomfortable and rude. It was whiteness that was complicit in its peacekeeping. It was whiteness that was evil in that moment. Whiteness was the thing that suffocated all the humanity out of each of us on that sunny summer afternoon, when all I wanted was a world where Black mothers could leave their sons with white mothers and know that we would keep them safe.

On Paradox, Shadow, and Light

That was the day I met a shadow side and became complicit in the system of white silence. Calling the place where our racism lives a "shadow side" is itself problematic. In discussions of whiteness and race, equating something bad with something dark like a shadow is a big part of our collective problem. This association of darkness with fear and evil is an image that is embedded deep within us. In a social construct that was borne of the Christian faith, in which whiteness is equated with holiness, people obsessed with our own goodness would, of course, be equally obsessed with our own whiteness.

I want at once to break down the association of "bad = dark" and "good = light" because of the way our stupid human brains will equate this to people and their skin. Like so many things about issues of race, the language we need does not yet exist; there is a paradigm void that we must work to fill. In a world where good guys wear white hats and bad guys wear black ones, human skin falls on a spectrum of shades that are meaningless apart from two things: their inherent beauty as an expression of God's diversity, and the structures of social hierarchy we place on them for the purposes of oppression.

My mother is a good person who stopped babysitting that little boy for his own good. But at the same time, she became complicit in a system that perpetuated racism, and she kept the racist in the room nice and comfortable. She is both good and racist at the same time, not because of malice in her heart but because of silence, systems, social mores, and institutions. She is a paradox.

Paradox is that strange place where two things are true at the same time. Often, the two things seem diametrically opposed. This idea that two things can be true at the same time is foundational to understanding good white racism. Statements like "You are a good person, and you are also a racist" are, essentially, paradoxes. The idea of paradox allows us to look and to see; it opens us up to the possibility that we may have something deep within us that needs to be rooted up, examined, and called to task. Very often, that truth is that despite our best efforts, people you and I would consider good (ourselves included) very often hold hierarchical thinking, placing more value on one thing than another. Paradox is important because once we embrace its existence, we can begin to journey into our shadow side.

This goes against everything we like to believe in America—and trust me when I tell you, it does nothing to simplify things. No one longs for simplicity more than I do, believe you me. But where we love to define things as—no pun intended—black and white, the truth is usually somewhere in the grey. Paradox is at the core of what I'm trying to say in this book—that crazy idea that a person can be both kind and kind of an asshole, all in one body. All in one minute.

Hell, any child of a certain age can prove *that* point.

We love things to be clear-cut, good or bad, one thing or another. Binaries like these make us nice and comfy-cozy because we can categorize and organize them easily into tidy little columns in our brains: good/bad, white/Black, racist/not racist. But this is like trying to hold water in a cardboard box. It may seem like a good idea until you understand that it won't work—and the truth of ourselves comes spilling out all over the place.

Binaries also prop up hierarchies. Jacques Derrida, a philosopher whose work I love (or maybe hate—I can't decide) shows us that any binary or dichotomy not only supports a hierarchy, but that the hierarchy will remain intact even if we flip the binary. I'm horrifically oversimplifying here, but stay with me, because it's important to understand as we move through the rest of the book.

Let's take the binary of white/nonwhite—you know, as a totally random example.

Whether you're ready to admit it yet or not, there's a hierarchy built in there. Everything about whiteness is perceived as better than nonwhiteness according to our hot little socialized norms. White is equal to "good guys," to "purity," to "closer to the divine." Nonwhite—regardless of the shade and its implications—is considered less than. Stained. Impure. Definitely not good. At least, not as good as white.

Derrida says that we can try to flip these binaries. Let's pretend for a New York minute that we're Jeannie from *I Dream of Jeannie* and, with a flip of our pretty blonde ponytail, we can all of a sudden reorder American civilization to a state in which whiteness is considered less than nonwhite. Whiteness is further from God; white represents impurity. White is bad. Nonwhite is now the thing to be.

The problem, according to Derrida, is that you have the same problem.

In his work known as deconstruction, Derrida says you need to burn that shit down, because the only way to get out of a binary is to deconstruct it, to tear it apart, to disassemble the pieces of it, examine them until your brain dribbles out your ears, and then rebuild something wholly different. Deconstruction allows us to see truth and also to reimagine something that is beyond our current reality.

Ultimately, this is my challenge to you and to myself—to reimagine a new way to be white in the world, to deconstruct the hierarchy and create a world in which everyone has enough and no one needs to be afraid.[3] You can call it what you want, but for me, this is what I think of when I hear the phrase "beloved community" or the "kin-dom of God." This book, therefore, is very much a manifesto of sorts, a call for us to begin to stretch our imaginings beyond the status quo, to dig deep into our creative coffers and pull out a new, beautiful thing. But before we can start that work, we must come to terms with an ugly truth: we may be good, but probably we are not as good as we like to think we are.

But America Is Good!

To understand where our American obsession with goodness comes from, I went to—where else?—the interwebz. There I found pop psychology and quizzes galore. But I also found myself swimming in the deep red sea of far-right conservatism, where toxic masculinity abounds and guns, missiles, and wartime heroes are all the rage. I hit gold in an article on the *American Thinker* website titled "A Case for America's Goodness" by Lloyd Marcus.[4] It's a perfect example of how both sides of the political spectrum love to oversimplify complex issues. The article starts off as a quaint description of an interview with a World War II veteran and ends in a red-faced rant about how America is not a racist country, with anecdotal evidence to prove the point. There are bold, generalizing statements that ignore nuance and claims of millennial leftist lies. At the end, Marcus concludes that "Americans are not racists"; in fact, he ends the article with the simple statement "Americans are good."

Americans are good.

In his July 2019 newsletter to his followers, evangelical leader James Dobson described a visit to the southern border of the United States during what can only be called an immigration crisis of epic proportions. After stating that many of the "illegals" who cross the border are "illiterate and unhealthy" and will overcome our culture, he states, "America has been a wonderfully generous and caring country since its founding. That is our Christian nature."[5] Except that there isn't a lot of Christ in what's happening on our southern border, and there isn't a lot of Christ in our history. What there is a lot of is oppression, injustice, slavery, torture. You get the gist. But according to certain faith leaders?

America is good.

Whereas Dobson seems to advocate a complete erasure of collective American memory, Marcus acknowledges the "sin" of slavery but bemoans the fact that anyone claims there has been racism in the time in between then and now, as if he'd rather skip over huge amounts of racial history like Jim Crow, redlining, the civil rights movement, events like the L.A. riots, and the murders of leaders of color like Martin Luther King Jr., Malcolm X, Fred Hampton, and the persistent killings of leaders within the Black Lives Matter movement. Marcus just wants America to be good, dammit. And he's willing to ignore, minimize, demoralize, and dehumanize whoever he needs to in order to maintain his chosen narrative.

As proudly as I adhere to progressive principles and beliefs, I'll also happily tell you that progressives in general don't handle the situation much better. We're quick to vilify conservatives, and we love to sound smarter than everyone else. Just as far-right conservatives can't seem to find it in their hearts to listen to people of color and the truth of their experiences, so progressives refuse to listen to very real pain and very valid perspectives of conservatives, including white ones. This is especially true in Christian circles, where we love to eat our own. Not only that, but we'll also get so excited about our newfound racial awareness that we'll go around explaining racism to the very people who experience it every day. We can be obnoxious like that.

At the same time, we have also been one of the biggest obstacles to antiracism work for civil rights leaders. Whether we're white feminists who want to ignore the realities of intersectionality that female BIPOC face, or whether we're tone policing people on social media, we place a huge STOP sign in front of activists and organizers, creating hurdles for the very people for whom we wish to be allies. When they call us on it, we get fragile and teary-eyed (or red-faced and defensive). We impede the progress of true antiracist work by paternalistically insisting that its proponents slow down and be polite; this is especially true in churches, where the work of social justice is often called "divisive." We're fine sharing a meme or two, but participate in an actual protest that disrupts the status quo? Well, that may be taking things too far. Everyone just needs to stop yelling and be nice. And we definitely need to follow the laws—even the unjust ones. We should be grateful for the progress we've made.

Except that for all that progress, *people of color are still dying*.

There is much in America of which we can be proud, but there is also much shame for us to bear. With the loss of nuanced paradox, our search for goodness has not left us good but rather unaware of our own evil. And I'll say it again: while we white people, conservatives and liberals alike, are over here yelling at each other, people of color are dying.

Literally *dying*.

Good people would not be okay with this. Since racism is generally understood by most good people to be a very bad thing, most good people don't want to admit when we're racist. In fact, we are so convinced of our own goodness that we can't even see our own racism. This is the construct I hope to dismantle in this book, by showing you that you can be a good person and still be hella racist. And you can be an even better person by admitting that fact, because that's the first step to doing anything about it.

Maybe as a collective psyche, we'll be able to start realizing that within all of us there can be both a hero and a villain, both honor and murderous intent, a side filled with light and a side without light, where our deepest, most agonizing pains might hide. If we in our collective identity can accept this, maybe we can practice some agency over it too.

The Psychology of Goodness

The good news is that when white people insist we're basically good, we're also basically right. We're not good because we are white, though. We're good because we are human. Despite the doctrine of original sin and all that fun, totally not-harmful-to-children-and-puppies jazz, science has made some significant discoveries that tell us we are, in fact, basically good. They can tell because of the way we make decisions.

We humans make decisions in two steps—the fancy name for this is *dual process framework*.[6] First, we use our *intuition*, then we enter a period of *reflection*, and research shows that the faster people make a decision, the kinder they are. The more time we have to reflect on the choice, however, the more self-centered and fearful we become.

Add unconscious biases to the mix, and things get really messy. The longer we spend in that time of reflection, the more unconscious bias has time to impact our behavior. It's important to understand that these impulses—first, the one toward kindness, and then the reflection period in which implicit bias appears— happen so quickly as to be virtually invisible to us. We think a thought, we feel a feeling, and then we act based on that emotion. Research shows that implicit bias is unconscious, very often even goes against our professed beliefs, and usually (but not always) preferences our own social group.[7]

Here's how it may work: imagine that you're a white person and you see a news story about an unarmed Black man who gets shot by a white police officer. Your very first reaction—one that you don't even notice—might be, "That's horrible." After all, most humans, unless you're a sociopath, will feel some sort of sadness when another human life is lost. That's the inherent kindness in you. Your next thought, however, will come from that implicit bias, fed to you from your diet of racist news streams, media, and perhaps even some personal narratives from family and friends. That thought—which you also don't notice—might be along the lines of "He must have done something to deserve it," even though there is no evidence to support that. Your only information is that an unarmed man was killed by an agent of the state. People who have had training in recognizing their implicit bias might be able to slow their thinking down and notice the narrative in their head, but many more of us will jump on Facebook and begin our campaign in support of the officer's innocence.

The thing is, the officer probably had a whole lot of unconscious bias happening in her head too. That's why she shot a man she was sure was a dangerous criminal who would hurt her if she didn't. Just like the rest of us, she's been programmed to believe in the inherent criminality and dangerousness of Black bodies, even if, in her everyday life, she has Black friends and hates the idea of racism as an ideology. In those split seconds when life and death are tenuously balanced on a heart-pumping river of adrenaline, her implicit bias will make the decision to pull the trigger before she can even apply rational thought to what's happening.

Since our brain's primary function is survival, we very quickly learn to categorize things into one basic binary: safe/unsafe. This helps keep us alive, but it also feeds our prejudices. As our growing brains are filled with images of stereotypes from media, scary news stories that tend to demonize certain groups over others, or even silent messages we get from our families of origin, our brains do the work of categorizing these images into the safe/unsafe binary. Anything unfamiliar, different, or other is deemed unsafe. In the milliseconds it takes for our brains to think a thought, we've already made a ton of decisions we're not even aware of based on unconscious bias—and that reflection period can impact how good we actually are in the world.

In other words, you may be a good person, and your first impulse may be kindness, but your brain is so filled with unconscious bias and weird categorizations that if you think about it too long, it'll make you do some very bad things.

Action Items

Learn: There are a number of amazing members of the BIPOC community who are doing excellent teaching on Instagram about the impact of whiteness. I suggest following these people: @rachel.cargle, @laylafsaad, and @nowhitesaviors. You might also go to implicit.harvard.edu and take a test to help you identify your own implicit biases.

Think: Does the idea that you may be racist while also being a good person make you uncomfortable? Are you willing to sit with that discomfort anyway? Why or why not? What makes this difficult for you? What would be different if you admitted you were a racist?

Act: Pay attention to conversations, newscasts, and people with whom you interact. When a thought appears in your mind that you recognize as inherently racist, write it down and question it.

Chapter Two

The White Empire

(Or, *You're Not White—You Just Think You Are*)

H ere is something I learned in acting school: No bad guy ever wakes up thinking he's the bad guy. Every villain in any script always thinks he's got a valid point. In fact, if he were telling the story, he'd be the hero—the good guy. It's natural to think of yourself as good and other people not so much. It's a theory I often try to remember in real life, when it comes to finding mercy for assholes. I don't always succeed, though. And of course, I'm fully aware that at any given minute I could be the asshole.

White people in America have trouble noticing when it's us who are the jerks in the room, and usually it's because we've been blinded by our own whiteness. When it comes to being white, it's important to understand that there is a difference between being a person with light skin and the monolith of whiteness. Whiteness is a complicated social identity that comes with a whole lot of cultural and political baggage—and all of it is privileged.

Still, just because I identify these as two different things—having light skin and an identity of whiteness—does not mean they operate separately in the world. They don't. If you are a white person, you carry this huge thing called whiteness not just on your back but in your very cells, in your neural pathways, in every conversation you have. Whiteness is your worldview, the lens through which you see everything, the empire in which you have citizenship. It's important to talk about the concept of empire and how whiteness operates within it, because empire and whiteness are BFFs, and they are also the mean kids in school.

And just like every bad teenage movie you've ever seen, even the bullies like to think they're good.

The Birth of the White Empire

Most of us—especially those of us who like to think of ourselves as good—sort of cringe at the idea of a white empire. It reeks of neo-Nazi imagery and white-hooded jerks carrying torches, and thankfully, most normal people find these images repulsive. But a white empire absolutely exists, and you and I—we're integral players in its game. So where did it come from? How did it start?

Empire happens when imperialist ideals and colonizing entities make babies. Imperialism is the ideological policy of a country that stakes a claim in dominating and ruling other nations; colonialism is the acting out of that ideal and those policies. Imperialism may be defined as ruling other countries through power, while colonizing specifically speaks to sending citizens of the imperial nation to the foreign land as "colonizers." (This is how the United States was born.) Regardless of what you call it, these ideals have at their core a very specific goal: to subjugate people and acquire land.

Empire is very much about land and resource ownership—specifically, ownership by a select few.

Like a lot of evil things that happen in the world, it all started with religion. To be fair, I don't think God had anything to do with it. Quite the opposite—it had to do with hubris and the human thirst for power. As the ruling religious body at the time, the church issued a number of documents that essentially gave "divine permission" to national leaders to go out and conquer the world. The Doctrine of Discovery was expounded in a series of official documents released by the church, starting with a papal bull from Pope Alexander VI in 1493 that specifically and intentionally gave divine right to Europeans to subdue, enslave, capture, steal from, and if necessary, murder the inhabitants of any land not currently dominated by Christians. These documents included inherently racist language that allowed leaders to dominate and oppress whole populations—most of whom were Black or Brown—and they called it the Lord's work.

Because obviously.

It is important to understand that these actions were believed to be *divinely justified*. The doctrine of dominion—a theological idea that claims the Genesis story gave dominion of the earth to human beings (*male* human beings, to be exact)—has been used to justify everything from male headship of the family to the desecration of forests in the Amazon.[1] *They* (white European men) were the ones to whom God gave dominion, and in their minds, that came with certain rights and responsibilities.

The European elites believed in their own proximity to God so much that they held that it was not just their *right* to conquer lands for Christ, but their *responsibility*. These Europeans *thought they were good*.

And the pope said, "God bless you, assholes. Go forth and prosper" (my translation).

By the time the first immigrants began to settle in the Americas, they carried with them the stories of "peaceful savages" that explorers had brought back to Europe with them. On the one hand, the indigenous populations were described as naturally barbarous and lazy, vicious heathens who were gluttonous to boot; on the other hand, they were considered simple and docile, a peace-loving people.[2] Given such stereotypes, the colonizers viewed their own motives—as messed up as we may think of them today—as good. They thought they were being kind, just, and godly by working to convert the native people. But even natives who "converted" were not allowed to intermarry with those of European descent, which demonstrates that ultimately skin color mattered—and the concept of race was born. Christian or not, dark-skinned people were considered less than human. As the United States was being born with lofty ideals of equality and freedom, ideas of group superiority were also being grafted onto the American vine of whiteness. And because whiteness was backed by power, the white empire was born.

Becoming White

As we look at the various waves of people groups who began to seek out American shores, you would think it would be obvious who was white and who wasn't. But that's not the case. It's very likely that if your ancestors weren't part of the original group of settlers, then at some point in your lineage, your great-great-great uncle wasn't considered white—or at least, not white enough. I'd love to be able to trace a nice, straight line to how each immigrant group became white, but I can't. The truth is that race is a fluid, contextual kind of thing that's not so easy to define, even if it seems like it should be as simple as looking at someone and seeing the color of their skin. After researching the history of immigration and trying to draw a clear progression from immigrant to whiteness, basically what I can tell you is this: it's complicated.

For many immigrants, racial status depended on who was in the room with them at any given time. A big part of the problem comes from the fact that the concept of race itself is a human fabrication—simply a way for us to categorize ourselves and others, specifically regarding access to power. Throughout history, the United States has had a difficult time defining race as new immigrant groups arrived and tilted the spectrum one way or the other. In the late 1700s, naturalization laws were confined to "free white persons" who were "fit for self-government."[3] This is important, because what that essentially means is that their right to vote, to have their voice heard in government, is based on an arbitrary assessment. In other words, as newer groups like the Irish—who were pale but not Anglo-Saxon—began to arrive, it became necessary to redefine and reclassify whiteness as (and I'm paraphrasing here): totally white, sorta white, not white enough, and hell no, you're nowhere close to being white.

As new immigrant groups arrived on American shores, they encountered the obstacles of empire—the solid systems made up of government, justice, education, and financial networks, just to name a few. But like empire tends to do, it also waved a golden carrot in front of their noses, luring them to assimilate with its promises of creature comforts and indoctrinating them in its ways. This assimilation came at the cost of their culture—they lost accents and cuisines, languages and music. They morphed into a cog on the wheel of whiteness as they moved their way up the hierarchy of jobs and status.

But they lost another thing too, and it's an important one. They lost a little piece of their humanity as they further separated themselves from the people who, because of the way they looked, could never enjoy the fluid racial status that those of a paler shade could. They separated themselves from their Black and Brown brethren, and they were glad for it, because the further away they were from them, the higher on the hierarchical rung they climbed.

White Tribalism

It's one thing to be categorized as white sociologically, to intellectualize whiteness and all its systems. Noticing these dynamics is important work, and it is something we must continually remind ourselves to do. But what does it mean for us personally when we realize we're not just light-skinned or Caucasian, but *white?* How does whiteness as a construct enter our psyche, and what does it do to allegedly good white people like us once it's there?

In many ways, it's about the power of the tribe—the way it controls our personal choices, develops our identities, informs our belief systems, and generally helps make us who we are. The tribe is a matter of survival—and it's an important one.

Deb Erickson, a coach I once worked with, explained it to me like this: From birth to the age of about seven, we quite literally depend on our family of origin—our tribal caretakers—for our very lives. Human children are incredibly vulnerable, and if our caretakers were to abandon or reject us during this time, we would die. Our brain is hardwired to focus on survival, so it will do absolutely anything to keep us in the tribe—even if it means picking up dysfunctional habits to please our parents so we can be safe from their rejection. The power of this survival mechanism is incredible and steadfast, and it's why you're still talking about your parents after ten years of therapy—your brain thinks it will literally die if you let go of the dysfunction they taught you. (No offense to parents out there. We all know parenting is hard, and nobody's perfect.)

It takes an incredibly strong, brave, and independent person to break free from the tribe—to go against the patterns of behavior and the roles you've been assigned to play in your family system. Trust me when I tell you that the thought of departure from those expectations freaks everyone out. They're not trying to be dysfunctional; they're just driven by the same biological needs for safety and security that you are. This neurobiology is crazy hard to overcome, and it's why so many white people cling to racist beliefs while claiming they're not racist at all. Any attempts to break free of the tribe-think makes your brain—and the brains of your loved ones—believe you're going to die. Your family or tribe will unconsciously think you're crazy and suicidal and therefore will act accordingly. So if you're feeling resistant to the content of this book, it's because your brain is going into safety overdrive, and it will take a strong act of will to overcome it.

A Bundle of Nerves

Right at the base of your skull is a pencil-sized bundle of nerves that's responsible, among other things, for deciding what information will make it into your consciousness. Our bodies and brains are bombarded with data and information constantly, and our focus and concentration cannot process all of it at once. The reticular activator is the filter that decides what's going to head straight to your subconscious to be filed away and what's going to make into your awareness.

Behavior doesn't just happen. First, you think a thought. Then, you have an emotion, and it's the emotion that drives your behavior. This happens hundreds of times a day, often without your awareness. You make decisions quickly, based on what the reticular activator has decided to let in. Because your brain is hell-bent on keeping you alive, one of its primary concerns is the relative safety of the stimuli it's assessing. Is this situation/thing/person safe? Remember from chapter 1 that the brain likes sameness.

This is the space in which implicit bias happens, and it happens quickly, automatically, and unconsciously. In fact, only 2 percent of our emotional cognition is available to us consciously; the rest happens below the radar, just out of reach of our awareness.[4] To intentionally change this takes slow, deliberate, conscious effort.

So why is this important in a conversation about race? Because you and I don't live in a vacuum. We live in a white empire, and that empire feeds us information to maintain the status quo, and we lick it up like a cat licks up milk. Implicit bias has both personal and institutional implications, and there is plenty of research that indicates it has a direct impact on social justice.[5] And remember: implicit bias can be positive (as in prowhite) or negative (as in antiblack). This can have direct consequences in a fear-filled, stressful scenario that requires quick thinking, like a shooting. A person who holds both prowhite and antiblack implicit bias will be more likely to shoot an innocent Black person and less likely to shoot a dangerous white person, all because of the way the synapses are firing in their brain.[6] A bad decision only takes milliseconds to make.

Think about the stories that society has taught you over the years. Think about the television shows you have watched, the books you have read, the products you have used, and the news you have watched. Most likely, even if your parents were the most inclusive, amazing, wonderful people you've ever encountered, you still consumed racist agendas. Whiteness surrounded you and easily became normative; it was the thing that simply *was*, so that anything that wasn't white was immediately different. Very likely, the Barbie dolls or the G.I. Joes you or your friends played with were white, except maybe for a token doll here or there. The holidays that were celebrated around you (whether you celebrated them or not) most likely included icons such as Santa Claus, who was probably white, or friendly "Pilgrims and Indians," in which the Pilgrims were white and kind and the Indians were incredibly happy to see them and share their corn. Even the damn Easter Bunny was never brown. Criminals tended to be Black or Brown; the good guys were always white. Magazines told you beautiful women come in only one color. All of these are examples of the ways empire reinforces white as normal and non-white as other. The other is confusing, different, and unfamiliar, and unless we're very careful (and we are rarely very careful) this difference quickly morphs into fear. When those narratives are backed up with personal stories, they are even more powerful.

White Fear

The trip down to Grandma's house in Metuchen, New Jersey, was always exciting. I loved imagining where my mom grew up, and on these trips, we'd drive through the old familiar town, past the house where she had lived. Often my mom would share stories from her childhood when her memory got triggered by a specific street corner or local store. One tale she told, however, I never forgot, and I can still remember the way it landed in my stomach as a pit of fear that had no place to go but my body.

Late one night she was driving home and stopped at a red light behind another car. Suddenly, a group of young men came out of nowhere, crossed the street, and surrounded the two cars. They put their hands on the hoods of the vehicles, and started pushing them up and down, as if trying to tip them over. Scared, my mother caught the eye of the man in front of her in his rearview mirror. He motioned that they should both go—just run the red light—which they did. My mom made it safely home to tell me that story many years later. But the one important detail she never forgot to include was that the young men who surrounded her car were Black. For some reason, this was important. To her, their Blackness seemed to have something to do with their intimidating behavior. Fear of Black men was implanted into my psyche at that moment, and it would reappear many years later when I was walking in a park near my house.

It's a beautiful park, and you can often find a bride walking randomly through the paths, hefting her long dress and long white train with a photographer trailing behind her. One day as I was walking, I saw a group of about seven Black men carrying bats. Immediately, I noticed that I was afraid.

My reticular activator fired up, showing me stories my mother and the white empire had told when I was very young, igniting the fear that had been instilled in my brain and cemented into my neural pathways. What didn't make it into my consciousness was the fact that the men were wearing tuxedos. The bats were tiny props, not full-sized, potentially deadly weapons. And they couldn't have cared less about me and my own little self. They were there to take some wedding pictures. Hardly a bunch of thugs on a wilding spree, these young men were smiling, laughing, happy, and completely nonthreatening to me.

What I felt was primal and visceral. I didn't just experience the fear in my head; it vibrated in my body, in my stomach where I'd once felt that pit of fear as I imagined my young mother being threatened in her car, alone save for a stranger in the car in front of her.

What I felt in that moment was tribal. It was the tribe of whiteness at work in my grey matter, in my energy patterns, in my neural pathways. It was not just the story my mother told me, but all the other programming my brain had encountered, from the normalization of white pseudosuperiority, to the stereotype of Black men as violent criminals that pervaded the images of my youth. Embedded in me like a viral code by both the white empire and my familial tribe of whiteness, this was the primal force of my survival brain at work.

Shame

Empire is an external thing: it's a force that exerts itself upon us, it's the sea we swim in, it's the invisible thing that raises us to be good little imperial foot soldiers. Our interpersonal (tribal) relationships often reinforce this; even among so-called nonracist families, racist tropes can become embedded in childhood psyches at a very young age. But if human beings are basically good, as we explored in chapter 1, then how does this happen without some serious internal discord?

Well, it doesn't.

In her book, *Learning to Be White*, Unitarian Universalist minister and theologian Thandeka explains how shame is a powerful
component of white identity, and it's the tool the tribe uses to
train up good white racists from the beginning. White shame,
according to Thandeka, is a set of "complex racial statements,
emotions and mental states . . . that [involve] the discovery of an
unresolved conflict . . . that, when discovered, make [white people]
feel flawed."[7] That conflict comes from parents.

Like my mother did when I asked questions about why we
couldn't babysit my new friend who seemed to upset our neighbor, Rudy, white parents often hush children who pointedly talk
about race, interact with people of different races, or otherwise
shake up the tribal lines. Children who have not yet internalized their own whiteness may show an outward curiosity about
skin color or hair texture that is free of malice, but white parents
will forcefully shut down their questions in an effort to maintain
their own comfort levels—because it's never comfortable for a
good white racist to talk about race. This results in internalized
shame in children, who feel the tension between what they want
(relationship with people of color) and what they need (protec-
tion offered by the tribe). The inner conflict here manifests in
a strange dichotomy of character in white people—on the one
hand, a steadfast belief that we are not actually racist; on the
other, blatant exhibitions of racist behavior and beliefs. This
paradoxical belief system develops because implicit bias often
goes against our conscious beliefs.[8] As we grow up to understand that racism is bad, we don't want to be associated with
it—remember that our first impulse is always toward goodness.
Our silence about racial issues enables us to believe that we are
not racist (e.g., "I've never said a racist thing in my life because
I've never said anything racial!"); meanwhile, our implicit bias is
working just under the surface as we make decisions on who we
will hire or fire, who we will socialize with, who we will judge as
guilty or innocent.

Our tribe is not just our families, though. We also participate in this thing called America, this strange experiment that
claims divine goodness as its core identity. I confess, though I am

critical of my country, I am also madly proud of it. I am proud of it because it created ideals in which I *could* be critical of it—openly and abundantly. America is a paradox itself, with its claims of liberty and justice for all, which it has never—not once—doled out equitably or generously. We have these founding fathers—dysfunctional, slave-owning bastards who were, at the same time, deep thinkers who were radically dedicated to human uplift (but mostly just for white people). How can these men—who some of us love to love and others of us love to hate—be both inspirational and atrocious at the same time? Because they were good white racists, so enthralled with their own sense of superiority that they could not see their own inhumanity, even when it was reflected back to them in the eyes of the people they owned.

Even if we like to think we're good—inherently, divinely good—we hold within our psyches a strange paradox of American white identity. It's an identity that claims idealistically that all people are equal but holds fast to a superiority complex that's so deeply embedded into our DNA that we hardly know it's there. We want to believe we are good, yet we know we have a lot for which to feel guilty. We are good people who participate in and benefit from a system that hurts other people, and it's all because of an accident of birth and the skin we climbed into when our souls left whatever place they come from and entered into being. We become, manifested, tools of the white empire.

Action Items

Learn: In order to deconstruct our own whiteness and build a new white identity, Ruby Sales says that white people need to dig into our cultural heritages, because we have been "flattened and homogenized." Seek to discover your information about your own heritage—what do you know about your cultural background?

Think: How did your family become white? When did your ancestors make the transition to whiteness?

Act: Make a list of some of the narratives you can recognize from your childhood that feed your own racist thought patterns. What have you learned from acknowledging them, and how will that cause you to act differently in the world?

Chapter Three

Gaslit and Ghosted

(Or, *They're Not Protesting the Flag— and You Know It*)

I started to post the question on Facebook and then I thought, *No. That's classic white laziness, to go to my friends of color and ask them to educate me.* So instead, I asked the expert on all things: Google. I typed "examples of racial microaggressions," and Google did not disappoint. It returned a plethora of examples, articles, websites, and resources about microaggressions and the harm they do. I confess that I felt myself relating in more ways than one. And some of those ways made me cringe.

This does warrant a confession, because as a white woman, I tread lightly when I say what I am about to say: that the microaggressions I've encountered as a *woman* helped awaken me to my own participation in microaggressions against *people of color*. This is a true statement, and it is a dangerous one. It's true because it is my story but dangerous because it could lead me to think I know what it's like to be a person of color. I don't.

Like, *at all*.

As a woman, I've experienced plenty of microaggressions, and they are exhausting. They are insidious and quiet. They often come wrapped in what is supposed to be a compliment, which puts you in the awkward position of feeling like you're supposed to say thank you for your own abuse. And they are so frequent that victims of them literally have to pick their battles just to survive the day. *Is this the one I confront? If I confront it, how will it affect my ability to remain employed, or live or work peacefully, or get home safely, or save this relationship that matters to me, or generally live in peace?*

The fact that, as a woman, I understand the impact of micro-aggressions does not mean that I am immune from participating in them against people of color as a white person. I once told an assistant of mine that I thought she was gorgeous—which was true. In my defense, we were close, and I was trying to be a supportive, encouraging sister. But I also said, "You're exotic, like a Mayan princess." Oy. She had emigrated here from El Salvador at a young age. This is the type of cringeworthy memory that makes me wish for a time machine so I could go back and shove a sock in my mouth or something. She just rolled her eyes, and a few weeks later, she and my other assistant, who was of half Chinese descent and half Hawaiian, brought me a basket of "exotic produce"—gorgeous fruits that were not part of my regular diet. Ha! A well-deserved touché that the me of fifteen years ago missed at the time. Now, though? I'm taking notes. I know I have perpetuated the same sorts of microaggressions against people of color that I experience as a woman—and I honestly never meant to. Now, I try to do better, and sometimes I'm successful.

Confronting microaggressions rarely ends well. It's often met with anger from the accused, and when this is a personal, in-real-life relationship, that kind of dynamic can get dicey. In fact, it can permanently ruin a relationship. The risk is very real for white people who step outside the norms of whiteness to confront its power and disrupt the status quo by pointing out racialized behavior in other white people. It's not just uncomfortable. We have a lot to lose, including relationships with family and friends who don't just mean the world to us but who are core to our sense of identity and security in the world. But every hero's journey involves stepping into the fullest version of ourselves, and I simply don't think white people can be our fullest, best selves if we are perpetuating racism.

Now that I'm aware of how my whiteness operates in any interaction I have, whether it's with another white person or with a member of the BIPOC community, it is imperative for me to pay more attention. To not pay attention is to exercise my privilege and power and do harm to others. To not believe people when they tell me about their experiences is to participate in evil. To insist that I'm not a racist while refusing to either pay attention or believe people makes me a good white racist. The first step to my own healing is to awaken to the psychological games that whiteness plays on the whole of society.

The Gaslighting of America

One of the ways microaggressions are both perpetuated and compounded is through a fun little form of psychological abuse called gaslighting.[1] If you've ever been the victim of gaslighting, you know the utter frustration of how it feels when it seems like you're living in an entirely different universe than everyone else. It's convenient, too, how that universe everyone else is living in seems to be one in which you're always wrong. Like, *all the time.*

Gaslighting is one of the tools that the white empire uses to keep marginalized people off kilter and oppressed. This happens time and time again, both interpersonally, in one-on-one interactions with white people, as well as on the larger, cultural, and sociological scale. I'll talk about the kind of gaslighting that happens in private, personal interactions later in this chapter, but we need to explore how sociological gaslighting occurs on a macrolevel first, because it demonstrates the size of the beast we're up against.

Scholars describe racial gaslighting as "the political, social, economic and cultural process that perpetuates and normalizes a white supremacist reality through pathologizing those we resist."[2] In other words, when a member of the BIPOC community points out racial abuse or injustice, the white empire will claim the act of pointing out the injustice as bad or unacceptable, rather than addressing the actual injustice. Suddenly everyone is talking about the person who pointed out the racist behavior, tearing them down, asking them to speak more softly, to stop being so sensitive—that maybe they are imagining things and should be nicer about explaining their hallucinations while they're at it.

Meanwhile, no one is talking about the actual problem—the racist behavior—because that is both uncomfortable and evidence that we might not be as good as we thought we were.

The result is that the white supremacist culture in which we all live is not just normalized but made downright invisible. By making the victims of the abuse seem evil, crazy, or out of control, we eliminate examination of the problem they are trying to point out in the first place and demonize them in the process. On a small, individual scale, this often plays out in microaggressions—small acts of oppression that seem hard to define but that have a huge impact on people of color. For example, a white woman might touch a Black woman's hair while telling her it's pretty. Though she's paying her a compliment, the white woman is also crossing multiple boundaries. When the Black woman points out the inappropriate behavior, the white woman will act defensive and innocent, and make it seem as if the Black woman is socially inept because she can't take a compliment. This is gaslighting at its finest.

Political scientists Angelique M. Davis and Rose Ernst have written about racial gaslighting in depth. According to them, gaslighters use the process of racial spectacle to help keep supremacist narratives hidden. A racial spectacle is an event or process in which the white empire is made invisible through the creation of ongoing cultural narratives that play out in both public platforms (e.g., media and politics) and interpersonal dynamics (e.g., your dinner table or Facebook feed).[3] It's important to understand, though, that not all racial discussions, whether public or private, are racial spectacles. Racial spectacles are only those in which the white empire or white supremacy is denied.

In their work about gaslighting and African American teachers, Tuesda Roberts and Dorinda Carter Andrews expertly lay out the structure of the gaslight relationship. It requires five components: the gaslighter (the abuser), the gaslightee (the person being abused), the object of manipulation (people or things used as the tools of manipulation), reward for the gaslighter (what the abuser gets out of it), and consequence for the gaslightee (end result for the abused).[4] Using this structure, let's consider a perfect example of cultural macrolevel gaslighting: the white racial spectacle that is the cultural response to Colin Kaepernick and the Take a Knee movement.

The Racial Spectacle of American Football

In 2016, pro football player Colin Kaepernick kneeled during the national anthem as a way to protest police brutality. The dissent sparked a movement, the consequences of which are still being talked about as I write this. However, the Take a Knee movement itself is not a racial spectacle—it is an act of resistance against the dominant powers at large. Its purpose is to call attention to the systems of injustice that Black people have endured and continue to suffer from to this day. The consequences of this injustice are undeniable, and the evidence is ubiquitous and easily researched, readily available for public consumption. This evidence points to the reality that Black lives are not valued by our society, and the Take a Knee movement exists to highlight this fact and bring it to the stage of national discussion.

The response to the movement, however, is a racial spectacle, because the counterarguments ("It shows disrespect to our flag and our military," "It is un-American," "It harms the ticket holders because they are subjected to a protest") all draw attention away from the actual racist system, hiding it beneath rhetoric that has nothing to do with the systemic racism and brutality to which Kaepernick originally wanted to call attention. While many white people, including myself, support the Take a Knee movement, multitudes of white people are incensed by it. In true gaslighting tradition, Kaepernick and others who support his public protest are demonized for calling attention to a deadly racial issue, and the furious response is not just illogical, *it intentionally misses the point.* By avoiding Kaepernick's *stated reasons* for protesting, Kaepernick's critics view him as some sort of national traitor, as unpatriotic, and as a hater of anyone who has ever served in the military. This narrative is merely a constructed reality designed to steal attention away from the actual problem—deadly racism—and toward the alleged victimization of . . . America? The flag? Soldiers? It's not exactly clear who is in danger as a result of some football players kneeling, and yet the response to these men has been as vicious as you might expect it to be if they'd been pedophiles. It makes no sense. I mean, in what context has kneeling ever been considered a threat? The association of Kaepernick's protest with disrespect of the military is a false equivalency that is typical of gaslighting.

Another critique I hear often is about how Kaepernick, as a celebrity, should keep his opinions to himself. The idea here was that he was being paid, and paid well, to entertain the masses (I'll talk about the consumption of Black bodies in later chapters), and since the average Joe doesn't get to spout his political beliefs at work, neither should Kaepernick. Meanwhile, celebrities who demonstrate acceptable patriotism—and not critique of the status quo—are celebrated as role models. A part of this critique about so-called workplace protest includes the false narrative that Kaepernick just wants attention and doesn't participate in any activism of import off the football field. (Of course, a simple Google search proves this wrong.) Finally, there is the simple, self-centered "I don't want to be subjected to that—I'm here to see a football game" argument, which is perhaps the laziest, most callous, and most disturbing critique of all.

According to the parameters set by Davis and Ernst, the Take a Knee movement is not a racial spectacle but a protest designed to illuminate the realities of police brutality in America. The white cultural response to the Take a Knee movement, however, *is* a racial spectacle, because what it seeks to do is not reveal racial inequity but rather to conceal the system of white supremacy by first demonizing the movement by claiming its intentions are anti-American and directed at the military, and second, by outright refusing to engage in a conversation about the brutal reality in which Black bodies must survive. It decides to yell louder about other things in the hopes that the whole race issue will just go away. It looks at blatant, murderous injustice, such as the shooting of Philando Castile, points the other way, and says, "Look! A squirrel!" and says the squirrel is more important.

Then it accuses the Take a Knee movement of being mean to the damn squirrel.

The squirrel—clad in a bedazzled stars and stripes tank top, no doubt—is then paraded in front of the public consciousness through talking heads on our newscasts and talk shows, and social media memes that are meant for us to forward without much thought. This image is reinforced in our private conversations and through our interactions with institutions of empire, such as our local police force. The squirrel becomes the narrative; meanwhile, Black people are still dying.

Now that we understand how racial gaslighting works, we can easily apply the five components that Roberts and Carter Andrews supplied to the Take a Knee movement. The gaslighter in this case is all the people who hate and criticize the movement. The gaslightee is Kaepernick and the people who support the movement. The objects of manipulation are the national anthem, American football, and the American flag. The reward for the gaslighter is the continued distraction from the point, which is police brutality, and the consequence for the gaslightee is the continued, exhausting effort that is required to constantly attempt to defend and explain their motives, which keeps them from ever talking about the actual issue at hand. Meanwhile, people are still dying.

Surprise! You've Been Gaslit Into Being a Racist

You may be surprised by the fact that there's another group of people who are the victims of racial gaslighting:

It's you.

And me.

It's us white people.

You and I have been gaslit into believing the false narrative of white supremacy, and it's been done with such expertise and skill that we don't even know it has happened. In fact, we will insist that it's not true, that we have not been the victims of gaslighting, thereby perpetuating this strange alternate universe that our abusers have created for us, where we're hella racist and all the while insisting that we're actually good instead.

I'm not for a second saying that BIPOC are not victims of gaslighting in both interpersonal relationships with white people and on a more macro, systemic level, because they undoubtedly are. What I *am* saying, however, is that good white racists like you and me have no idea how we're tools for the empire—and that's how gaslighting works.

So who is this unnamed abuser who is manipulating white people into being tools (in every sense of the word)? It's those first Europeans who went out and stole lands and enslaved whole people groups, believing it was the will of God. They have passed down to us a generational trauma. It's the overt racists who used racial spectacles such as lynchings and cross burnings and tiki torches and swastikas to instill fear into our ancestors, our parents, and yes, even us. It's the people who hushed us when we were children wanting relationships with people of color. It's the capitalist society that uses Black and Brown bodies to sell us pancake mix and rice, telling us it's totally okay to consume Aunt Jemima and Uncle Ben for our own pleasure and comfort and telling us that it's wholesome nourishment. It's absolutely the megawealthy who have knowingly devised political plans to keep us poor and separate so we won't get in the way of their greed and avarice. Plans such as the Southern Strategy are carefully executed methods that both play to our inherent racism and reinforce racist ideas through carefully constructed racial narratives that become embedded in our brain cells and neuropathways until we believe them as truth. To resist feels not just futile but dangerous to our well-being.

Key to Davis and Ernst's definition of gaslighting is that it focuses its efforts on those who resist. Think back to the previous chapter where we discussed the way racial shame is embedded into a white child by parents who quiet the child's racial curiosity. In this case, the child represents resistance to the supremacist status quo and is made to feel othered and wrong by the child's own family of origin—the ultimate in gaslighting technique. Think about how Donald Trump claims to want to "Make America

Great Again" by playing on a fear that we will lose something precious if we don't protect what we have from Brown-skinned people crossing the border. This is how whiteness and white people become, at once, both gaslighter and gaslightee in one perfectly horrible racialized system.

Let me be clear: though I hold the opinion that white people have been gaslit into being racist jerks, I don't think this for one second lets us off the hook. The purpose of this section is not to let you say, "Oh, well, I've been the victim of gaslighting, so therefore I don't have to do anything about it." No way. What I'm trying to do is shake us out of the spell that's been cast over us, to get us good and pissed off about it, because I know that like me, if you're a good person, you don't want to be a racist. You don't want to knowingly participate in a racist society. You don't want to benefit from a privilege you didn't earn. I'm telling you that you've been manipulated by the powers that be, and they like to stay invisible. I'm pointing to them and telling you that they have gotten you to play in a system that you'd not willingly choose. I'm holding your face and opening your eyes and telling you to *look*.

Using the steps that Roberts and Carter Andrews lay out, let's break down the Take a Knee movement into the appropriate gaslighting roles, and we'll see how average white Americans—the people I'm calling good white racists—are being manipulated through classic gaslighting techniques to perpetuate racism.

The gaslighter in this case is the white empire—all the networked systems and institutions, such as the media and the justice system, the government and the entertainment machine in the form of the NFL—that work together to manipulate the masses. The gaslightee is not in this case the Black population. The harm done to the Black population is undeniable and inexcusable, but generally speaking, they don't need a white person to tell them it's happening.

Rather, the Black population (or more specifically, the Take a Knee movement) is the tool of the gaslighter, the object of manipulation that the gaslighter uses to perpetuate the system and the status quo. It uses the movement by demonizing it, giving the process something tangible to point to as evil and distract the gaslightee from the real injustice, from the actual Very Bad Thing—the consistent murder and oppression of our fellow human beings that any good person should be enraged about. Another tool is the military—a diverse population of individuals, some of whom are (brace yourselves) actually Black and some of whom may actually agree with Kaepernick. The national anthem and the American flag are also tools in this game, symbols that the system uses to garner allegiance and high emotion in order to evade the intense lament and despair that is the appropriate response to the unjust and systemic murder of people in the BIPOC community.

The gaslightee is the white person who has bought into the racial spectacle hook, line, and sinker—the anti-Kaepernick propaganda—because their perception of reality has been altered, reconstructed to believe that a person who resists the ongoing murder of their siblings is somehow evil, or wrong, or at the very least unpatriotic. Let's ignore the untold number of deaths of our fellow humans at the hands of the state and instead point to "Black-on-Black crime," as if that were even a thing, as if it would suddenly make what happened to Sandra Bland or Freddie Gray totally okay, or at least unimportant. We do this because we have been manipulated. And I don't know about you, but it pisses me off to think that I might somehow be duped into thinking that being angry about the unjust murder of my fellow Americans makes me or anyone else unpatriotic.

In the case of cultural gaslighting around the Take a Knee movement, the reward for successfully manipulating the nation is the maintenance of the status quo, the sustained power and dominance of the white empire. If white people demonize those who resist their own destruction, whiteness can maintain its position at the top of the hierarchy. The consequences are the continued oppression of Black and Brown people and the perpetual participation in racist systems by white people who like to consider themselves good. After all, racism doesn't require us racists to understand our own white supremacy in order to be effective. We don't have to be aware of our bias. In fact, it's our lack of awareness—our insistence that we're actually good people—that makes us extra good at being racist jerks.

Defensive AF: When White People Are Confronted with Our Own Racism

So what is it about the Kaepernick protests that elicits such rage and disgust from so many white Americans? Why do we go to such lengths and participate in such mental gymnastics in order to maintain the status quo and ignore the plight of our fellow citizens? According to psychologist Dacher Keltner and writer Jeremy Adam Smith, it's because Colin Kaepernick messed with our collective rituals. He stepped out of his role in the tribe, and it freaked us all out.

In an article in *Scientific American*, Keltner and Smith say that Kaepernick's actions turned a collective ritual—the playing of the national anthem—into a somber reminder of our own shortcomings when it comes to the American dream.[5] Our amygdalae—the part of our brain associated with emotions—are activated by Kaepernick's protest, and we're alerted to the fact that he's deviated from tribal norms and group tendencies. Our reticular activators start screaming "Danger! Danger!" whenever a player's knee hits the ground.

I agree, and I add that like Thandeka's shame-based theories, Keltner and Smith's idea suggests that not only do we all know how far we've fallen from actually fulfilling the American idea of equality and justice for *all*, but we're so obsessed with the collective narrative of American goodness that we will deny what we all know in our bones to be true *because we cannot imagine how to fix it*. We are ashamed of our failure of imagination when it comes to healing ourselves and our country's racial problems, so we prefer to pretend everything's fine—and we will ideologically eviscerate anyone who tries to say otherwise.

It's not fun to be confronted with your own racist behavior, and it's definitely not comfortable. For good white racists, talking about race causes a psychic discord, because hidden beneath our positive self-images and our ideological Americanism is a deep river of shame—shame over the brutality of our ancestors, shame over the inhumanity of our skin-kin, shame over the privilege we know we enjoy while others do not. The problem with the maintenance of our own comfort is that it prohibits us from seeing the very brokenness we need to heal. Like any fully dysfunctional family system, our shame keeps our chins defiantly high in a faux defensiveness, in the hopes that no one will notice what everyone sees—that we have reparations to make. Ultimately, I believe we are afraid that if we confess our shame and lay it bare for the world—and people of color—to see, they will show no mercy. We are afraid of what reparations might look like.

In our defense, though, I acknowledge that the plight of racism is overwhelming, even for those of us who are trying hard to stare it down directly. I think many good white racists, when we allow ourselves to really examine the matter in the deeper recesses of our minds, might recognize the injustice and feel overwhelmed and at a loss as to what to do about it. We have tried to live our lives as best we can; we have tried to treat everyone equally; we have tried to be kind and good and generous. When we look at the history of our nation and our people, something inside of us withers and cringes at the cruelty of white supremacy, but damned if we know what to do about it. So instead, we raise our chins, search for justifications and denials, and say, "Not my ancestors."

But our defensiveness only perpetuates the reality that our success, our lifestyle, our happiness, and, yes, even our perceived goodness as Americans were built on the backs of people who were kidnapped, enslaved, tortured, pillaged, and/or slaughtered. Even if it's true that your ancestors never owned slaves, what's also true is that you, if you are assigned an identity of whiteness, benefit from the system that was created around slavery—a system that makes it easier to glide through life in white skin. Good people who care about our fellow human beings—good white racists who are healing from deep psychic injury—acknowledge this. We own it. We work some version of the 12-step program for racists, making "a searching and fearless moral inventory of ourselves"[6] and paying attention daily to our cravings for power, comfort, and our perceived goodness.

The Four D's

It's funny how people poke the beast and then get insulted when it growls. I see this defensiveness up close and personal on my Facebook page. I'm a pretty straight up, what-you-see-is-what-you-get kind of person. I suck at being fake, and the amount of energy it takes for me to try just isn't worth it. Like everyone else when it comes to social media, I tend to post my highlight reels and not the worst stuff, like the fights with my husband or the way I look most days or the strange stickiness that seems to pervade every surface of my home. (I have children, which should explain everything.) But one thing you'll learn about me right away, after just one look at my Facebook pages or my Instagram feed, is that I talk about race, I talk about white people, and I support movements like Black Lives Matter and Take a Knee. I do not hide this. This is as obvious as the color of my hair and the fact that I am a Jesus freak. I let this all hang out like my grandmother's underwear on a clothesline. Still, white friends and acquaintances will reach out to me, challenge me on some aspect of my beliefs, then act both surprised and hurt when I call them out.

Based on multiple experiences, I have noticed a very definite pattern to conversations about race with white people—especially those who claim to be really good people and, of course, totally not racist. This pattern involves what I call the Four Ds (there are actually five, but the first two go together, and I was never good at math anyway): *deny/detract, distract, disclaim,* and *disappear.* Let's break down each one of those and look at why it's a problem.

Deny/Detract

This phase of the conversation usually comes first and is a knee-jerk reaction by white people when confronted with the idea that a situation might have racist overtones. Essentially this is an intellectual and emotional rejection that racism is happening, and it manifests as some sort of minimization, justification, or excuse for the racist behavior. Here's when you'll find white people saying stuff like, "Oh, they probably didn't mean it that way," or "Don't you think you're being a little sensitive? Why does *every-thing* have to be about race?" or the perennial favorite, "Not all white people."

I confess that sometimes I do this too; on better days I practice some agency over it and use my internal filter like a grown-up before I let my stupidity fly. Because white people live in a world in which our racial identities are normalized, we don't often have to think about racial dynamics and the way they operate in a social setting. We don't have to think about what sorts of microaggressions people of color may be enduring as we sit beside them at dinner. We don't have to scan a room for its vibe the way BIPOC do. Just like men don't consider their own safety, for example, when they walk down the street at night like women do, white people simply don't need to worry that our whiteness may put us in danger, whether physical or emotional. The fact that we don't think about it leaves us open to participating in racist behavior inadvertently. But it also makes it difficult for us to see racist behavior or situations for which we or other people are responsible.

I cannot tell BIPOC that they should accept behavior they are experiencing as oppressive. Even in close relationships with people of color, our whiteness is at play at any given time, and we may not be aware of it. I can't speak for BIPOC, but I think it is potentially far more costly—in trust equity, in emotional health—for them to be in close relationship with us. What feels equal and fine to us may feel more like a minefield for them; the field might be beautiful and blooming with the colors of spring, but buried underneath those tall, lush grasses may be a bomb that will blow them to bits. We may accidentally be that bomb. Our good intentions as white people do not automatically mean that our behavior is harmless. Good people should want to be aware of this.

Why It's a Problem

As the first and foundational step in the gaslighting process, the refusal of white people to acknowledge that racism is happening not only inhibits our own healing, but it is abusive to the person we are diminishing and sets the stage for further abuses as the interaction continues. If the conversation is with a member of the BIPOC community, it tells that person, who is expressing a response to their own abuse, that refusing to be abused or calling out abusive behavior is somehow a bad thing.

It prioritizes the comfort of white people—who'd rather talk about anything but race or, even worse, our own whiteness—over the pain of the person who just suffered injustice. This demonstrates that we white people are more concerned with our own comfort level than we are with affirming people of color and their experiences with racism. Because maybe it's not all white people, but it's probably most white people, and it's definitely enough white people to make it a really big problem. And if you're saying, "Not all white people," you're probably one of those white people.

Distract

This is the part of the conversation in which the good white racist starts making all sorts of claims that divert the focus of the conversation away from the injustice and toward something that blames and demonizes people of color in order to maintain her own perceived goodness and comfort level. Rather than talk about the overwhelming evidence that people of color are subject to radical injustice, white people will instead say things like, "But what about Black-on-Black crime?" or "If he had just obeyed the cop's commands and not been so angry, he never would have gotten shot," or "I don't get paid to protest. They should protest on their own time, not when I've paid good money for a game. And besides, kneeling during the national anthem is disrespectful to our military."

Why It's a Problem

These distraction techniques are absolutely exhausting, which may, indeed, be the point. If we can scream and yell and throw a red-faced tantrum about all the things that don't actually mean anything instead of addressing the actual problem of racial injustice, we can maintain our own comfort level and never have to do the deep work of unpacking our own white shame. This perpetuates the injustice and deadly reality that people of color must deal with daily, and it maintains the demise of our own souls as we continue to bolster this injustice with illogical arguments. We lose our own humanity in the process, or at least, all the things that make being human worth it: mercy, compassion, critical thinking, and basic common sense. This is a price I am no longer willing to pay.

Obviously, it is also harmful to our siblings of color. When we refuse to acknowledge the pain of others, we compound it. We leave them feeling frustrated, abandoned, hopeless, and angry. It is, at the very least, inhospitable to change the subject when a person is expressing pain or anger. At worst, it's manipulative and cruel.

Disclaim

Here is where good white racists insist upon their own goodness due to their proximity to people of color. In other words, *I'm good and totally not racist because I've dated a lot of Black men / my best friend is Black / I adopted a kid from China / I work with inner city youth / I'm a cop, so I know about Black-on-Black crime.* These disclaimers use relationships with people of color as some sort of absolution, as proof of one's goodness, because people of color would never be in relationship with a racist. Often in this conversation a good white racist will proudly state that he and his Black friend regularly talk about race, and the person of color *always affirms him.* This may or may not be true, but it's also like saying that famine and hunger are not a global problem because there's food on your plate at dinnertime. It's not universally true, and it's also totally not the point.

Very often such relationships not only make good white racists feel good about ourselves, but they also make us feel overly confident in our knowledge of the Black experience (or the Korean experience, or the Puerto Rican experience . . .). Now not only are we good white racists absolved of any racism because of these relationships, but we're also *experts* on race.

Why It's a Problem

This is a myopic view that proves nothing other than you have generous friends who happen to be of color. The fact that I have friends of color does not remove the fact that I'm a good white racist who needs to check my thoughts and my behavior daily. It doesn't change the fact that almost every time I do, I'm disappointed with myself. Using my BIPOC friends to prove I'm not a racist is tokenism at best. It's using people we say we care about as props to create a universe in which we are always good. At worst, it's a way to ignore or excuse our own racism and let us off the hook. It removes the need for us to do the work of imagining a better way to be.

Disappear

This is the sad truth of almost every conversation I've ever had with white people about race: eventually, we disappear. I know I've done it, and others have done it to me. When the conversation gets too uncomfortable, when we're not coddled and let off the hook, when people refuse to let us hijack the conversation, we simply vanish from the conversation. Sometimes we vanish from whole relationships.

In our defense I will say this: while the way in which we do it (usually, through unhealthy ghosting or radio silence) often sucks, sometimes our disappearance is for very healthy reasons. I was once in an online antiracist group led by a Black woman in which there was a lot of justified anger being expressed by BIPOC. It was a difficult space to be in, because even though I knew I was not personally the target of much of the fury, I also knew I represented its cause. It was hard not to be triggered, not to type in all caps, "NOT ALL WHITE PEOPLE." When I was personally called out for a racist comment, I struggled to understand why what I said was racist, and while I did not remove myself from the group, I did become quiet, and simply observed. It was a time of deep learning for me, as I began to experience what it was like to roll around in the depths of my internalized racism. It was uncomfortable and not something I wanted on full display for the world to see. But it was also deeply fruitful, because it ultimately led to antiracist work in my own psyche and in the world.

But not all disappearances are healthy, nor do they lead to antiracism. Very often they are escapism, an attempt by a white person to reject learning in favor of comfort. When I talk about white people disappearing, I'm not talking about when they're digging deep and doing the work. I'm talking about when white people leave the conversation to return to their echo chambers, where they are only affirmed and never challenged to consider the possibility that they may not be entirely good. I've seen white people unfriend me on Facebook at a moment's notice if the conversation gets too real for them. None of this behavior is about self-reflection; it's about deflection and denial.

Why It's a Problem

It's a problem because by disappearing, we break the very first rule of antiracism work: *stay in the room*, even when it gets hard and uncomfortable. Staying in the room is not about centering yourself and your pain. It's about learning and being willing to stand in the rage and fury of BIPOC and not take it personally. It's about holding space for our fellow humans who deserve their chance to grieve and rage and weep and mourn. It's about doing that ourselves, in the appropriate time and place, when we can do so without centering our whiteness. Leaving robs us all of hearing and being heard, of learning and teaching, of growing together and creating the kind of solidarity it will take to heal our souls and the world. If you need to process, do so. But have enough grace and etiquette to say, "I'm struggling with what you're telling me. This is hard for me to hear. I'm going to stay in the room, but I'm going to be quiet now, to process and to learn. Please don't take my silence as disappearance. This matters to me, and I am still here."

The Four Ds in Action

Consider how the Four Ds played out in a conversation I had online with a white woman. It's a perfect example of the good white racist preoccupation with maintaining our own comfort and defending our own goodness—and also of the inexplicable way people think that I'll suddenly change my mind and coddle their whiteness if they object to what I'm saying. (I've changed identifying details to protect privacy.)

I'd posted a meme on Facebook that said, "Rosa Parks was not protesting the bus. Gandhi was not protesting the food. The players are not protesting the flag or the troops. They are protesting injustice."

The meme got the usual likes by the usual folks. One friend, however, was the first to comment. She agreed, but wanted to know what the players do in the off-season and where this was covered in the media. Note how she was refusing to enter into a meaningful conversation about the actual injustice the meme was pointing to, choosing instead to focus first on attempting to demonize the players for not doing enough about said injustice, and second, to demonize the media for not covering the additional work the players should be doing about said injustice. The injustice itself was ignored. A detract/distract double whammy!

I was not in the mood to coddle that day, and so I responded to her question honestly and completely. I explained that drawing attention to what the players do or don't do off the field is a distraction, and that protests are meant to be disruptive. I told her that Martin Luther King Jr. and other civil rights leaders often heard the same kind of critique from their detractors—that is, of their methods—rather than a response to the actual problem the movement was protesting. I pointed out that she was participating in a classic system of silence and oppression by insisting on changing the subject to what Kaepernick does in his time off the field (though I did go ahead and share a link to his nonprofit).

Her response was quick and frail. She claimed it was a valid question (which was easily answered by a quick Google search, had that really been what she was curious about) and then accused me of "tearing her apart." Though my response was thorough and yes, brutally honest, it also wasn't about her at all. It was a critique of the argument she posited and was designed to guide her back to the point—which she never actually did get to. Rather than addressing the injustice, she centered herself and her perceived victimization (i.e., being "torn apart").

I replied with an invitation to enter into a conversation about the point of the protest: police brutality. Instead, she moved onto another of the Four D's—the disclaimer: "I have plenty of conversations with strong Black women, and I'm totally comfortable asking my friend questions and sharing my point of view." Then she wanted to end the conversation—the one she started—because "she loves me as a sister in Christ."

I could not help but notice that she says she feels 100 percent comfortable asking her Black friend questions and sharing her point of view, and I was reminded of something I learned from my friends of color once: "If the white people in the room are happy and comfortable, chances are the people of color in the room are not." I told her that I was glad she was in relationship with strong Black women, but I also pointed out that one of the ways she could be a better friend would be to do her own work.

Her response was to assure me that her friend is totally fine with it because they "learn from each other." While this may indeed be true of their relationship, it's dangerous for white people to always assume that our friends of color are totally okay with being our racial educators. When Google is a thing, it's always safer to go there first. It's not like there is a shortage of materials from which to learn about this topic. Amazon and Barnes & Noble are also—surprise—great resources. The point is that the BIPOC community does not owe us an education.

Then my friend pulled out the big guns: "My dad's family from five generations ago was African, brought over as a slave. I have been in touch with my roots and know how my family has dealt with race over generations."

More disclaimers! Because five generations ago there was an African in her lineage, my white friend understands racism. Except for the whole part where she's totally white—where she has been assigned whiteness as a social location in America and has enjoyed all the benefits and unearned privileges that go with that identity.

I continued to try to get her back to the topic. I told her the point of the protest is that Black people are dying in inordinate numbers. Our conversation was diverting the attention away from the problem and centering the attention on us—white women. "Maybe," I said, "we could talk about the issue at hand, which is police brutality?"

And POOF! She was gone. She disappeared from the conversation, never to return again. We never did have a discussion about the actual point, and a few weeks later I noticed that she had unfriended me on Facebook. That's a shame, because I genuinely liked her.

I know this is uncomfortable. I know it's not easy. But we don't have time for white tears and frailty. White people need to pull up our big kid underpants and rally—if we really want to be good, that is, if we really want to create an America that is actually great, that actually lives up to its own ideals. We don't have time to coddle our feelings. We have work to do.

Because the time is urgent.

People are dying.

Action Items

Learn: Do some research on the Take a Knee movement, and learn what Colin Kaepernick's foundation does and why it matters to the people it serves.

Think: Have you ever participated in the Four Ds when confronted with a racialized conversation? How did you feel? Were you escaping, or were you retreating to do the work? What did you learn?

Act: Next time you are confronted with a racial conversation, *stay in the room* and see what happens.

Chapter Four

The Power of Language

(Or, *Are You Freaking Kidding Me? No, You Can't Use the N-Word*)

Let's get right to the point here: If you're white, *hell no, you can't use the N-word.* Stop pouting about it, for Pete's sake. And if you are a white person who likes to consider yourself good, I can't imagine why you'd even *want* to. But—surprise, surprise— there are five hundred boatloads of white people who do, at least when they're singing along to their favorite songs, and not only do they want to, but they get all hurt and whiny when someone tells them they shouldn't.

Before you say it—no, this isn't about equality or the right to free speech. I mean, you can go ahead and exercise your "rights" and use the word, but let's be clear about something first: if you do, consider it your turn to be the asshole in the room. Also, get your "good white racist" T-shirt out, because you're representing loud and clear.

We'll get to the specifics on white people using the N-word and other fun racially charged entitlements in a bit, but first we need to examine why this is so important. Why a whole chapter dedicated to language and the way we use it to perpetuate our status as good white racists?

Language Is Power

Language is the mechanism by which we express our innermost existence, the actuality of ourselves and our being. In this way, language is *our* power; it is the way we manipulate the air around us to make the mark of our own being in the world. At the same time, language has power *over* us; it is the thing that is used to define us, to empower or disempower us, to assign value to our existence or deny it. Language is the foundation on which personal identities are built, societies are constructed, governments are empowered, and institutions are centered. But language is also something else: it's an agreement.

Together we agree upon meaning. This social contract is subtle; we don't always consciously enter into it or realize our own intentionality when we allow words to become symbols for the realities they represent. Instead, we simply absorb it, learning the complexities and subtleties of meaning as we go. We also rarely think about the limitations of language—that it can never completely capture the fullness of its own meaning. Symbols are lackluster when you compare them to the actual realities they represent.

Language is contextual—a meaning may be appropriate in one setting and not appropriate in another. When you start to really pay attention, you can begin to see that the hierarchies we talked about in chapter 1 exist because of language. Language creates these power structures, the unequal binaries that create categorical meaning in our brains.

By using our voices, we can resist empire or be complicit in it; in turn, empire can silence us as a means of disempowerment, as a way to deny our humanity, our culture, our identities. Empire defines us by the way we use language; it classifies us as intelligent or not, worthy or not, welcome or not, depending on our mastery of one language or another. Language has been weaponized by empire, used to squash entire movements or people groups. One of the first ways empire works to absorb and assimilate a people group into itself is to require the use of its own language and the death of indigenous tongues. Empire has done this almost everywhere it goes. And because language is ubiquitous and always malleable and fluid, meanings change but etymologies don't, and soon perfectly good people are using words that are inherently racist, without even realizing the consequences.

Even the word *racist* exerts power, and you can confirm this by noting the way your stomach feels every time I insinuate that it's possible you might be one. The word *racist* has been imbued with such a visceral, strong, and negative meaning that the thought that it might describe you makes you feel defensive, hurt, and probably even angry. It makes you want to stand up and shout, "I'm not a racist!" It makes you feel a certain way. The social collective has agreed that racism is bad, but rather than acknowledge how what we just said or did may have been racist (intentionally or not) and how it harms members of the BIPOC community, good white racists will instead focus on their hurt feelings about being identified as racist. That's the power of language.

In and of itself, if you're feeling a certain way about being called a racist, that might be reason enough for not using the N-word—like, *at all*. But whatever.

Language as Torture Device

Language is so indelibly entwined with our identities that empire uses it quite effectively in torture—or rather, empire uses torture to *remove* language from victims, reducing them to a prelingual state in order to appropriate their voices. In her book *Shattered Voices: Language, Violence, and the Work of Truth Commissions*, Teresa Godwin Phelps clearly lays out the process of language removal through torture on a personal, familial, and societal level. Though her work specifically looks at dictatorial regimes in South America—renowned for their barbarism—the process she lays out can be applied (over a disturbingly long time stretching generations) not just to slavery but even today, to the way we continue to use language to oppress entire people groups, especially groups of color.

According to Phelps, torture is the ultimate exercise of power.[1] Physical pain is an experience that is impossible to fully express. When my shoulder hurts, I can tell you about the pain, but you can never fully understand it; it is a wholly personal and subjective experience. But this inexpressibility makes it a perfect tool for political use through torture, because the victim is reduced to the unutterable: screams and moans that are heard by no one but the abuser. The real purpose of torture is to dismantle the victim's identity and render her languageless. When reduced to this infantile state, the victim is removed from any semblance of participation in society; there is no longer a sense of solidarity with the world. Rather than authentic confession, empire, through torture, appropriates the now disembodied voice, using it to speak the message of empire—think of how many times we have heard recorded messages by prisoners of war that praise the captors. The power of this kind of torture, and the reason the victims resent it so much, according to Phelps, is because it is not only horrific and painful but is also a symbolic message that communicates superiority of the wrongdoer over the victim, a lesson that says clearly who counts and who is irrelevant.[2] State-sanctioned torture affects society as a whole. Count one human life as less than or unworthy, and we devalue the inherent worth of every citizen.[3] If a government does nothing to stop the ongoing torture of its citizens, its silence and inaction is paramount to approval. If the citizenry at large does not hold that government accountable for its sanctioned use of torture and dehumanization, that citizenry is just as complicit.

It is not surprising that Phelps discovers in her examination of torture victims a desire for revenge. But what is surprising is that this first impulse proves ultimately unsatisfactory. What victims really want is their voice back—they want their story told and affirmed. They want the air to vibrate with the memory of their screams, for the truth of their agony to be affirmed.

It is not an easy or by any means a pleasant trip to make, but we can journey through American history and easily discover that, as a society, we have never stopped using torture against the BIPOC community, especially in the form of linguistic oppression. There is no doubt that we colonized First Nations people by stealing their children and beating their native language out of them, wanting to "kill the Indian to save the man." There is no arguing the fact that enslaved Africans were kidnapped and tortured, or that their identities were decimated by the removal of their names and languages. White people carry the whip of persecution in our very DNA, passed down through generation after generation. Separated from our brethren of color by the lashes our predecessors doled out, we continue to participate in the practice of racial silencing, to steal and silence voices of color, appropriate them, and stuff the words of empire into their mouths like a smelly rag.

Like the secret, white-hooded members of the KKK who rode through the night to anonymously light their crosses afire, we practice a similar type of cowardice when we refuse to give BIPOC people the right to use their voice, whether they are protesting on a football field or in the streets of Ferguson, Missouri. Every time we tone police a Black person who is angry about injustice, or a First Nations person who is crying out for equity and truth, or a Latinx person crying out for recognition, we are perpetuating the torture committed by our ancestral lineage—by the tribe of whiteness. We participate in emotional torture every time we refuse to listen, every time our news media ignore violence against the BIPOC community, every time we look away from the part we play in the school-to-prison pipeline or the addiction rates on reservations. Every time a family is refused justice for a murdered son or daughter, we participate in the continued torture of our siblings of color.

What White People Don't Understand:
White Ignorance, Code Switching, and AAVE

Another way that language is a tool of empire—and a way that good white racists wield that tool with expertise—is through our subtle judgment of languages we don't understand. Whether it's our belief that people speaking Spanish are somehow less American, or the way we have collectively decided that Black English denotes lesser intelligence, the Standard American English most good white racists speak has become weaponized, a tool used in oppression and the maintenance of the status quo. If you're wondering how that might be, consider your own reaction when you hear a Black person who doesn't "sound white," and pay attention to the subtle judgments you make about that person. Do you consider him less intelligent? Less educated? Would you hire him?

The fact is that scholars have determined that African American Vernacular English (AAVE) is a complex and completely valid form of English; it simply has rules and vocabulary with which the average white person is unfamiliar. In other words, Black people who speak both AAVE and Standard American English are, in a sense, bilingual.[4] In most white circles, that would make them pretty damn smart. But we have different standards for different skin.

Meanwhile, white insistence that people in the BIPOC community speak Standard American English—and our refusal to recognize AAVE as a valid dialect in and of itself—has real life-and-death consequences. During the trial of George Zimmerman for the murder of Trayvon Martin, key witness Rachel Jeantel, who was the last person to speak to Trayvon before he was killed, was verbally eviscerated in the press and on social media by people who decided she was dumb. She spoke AAVE, and immediately her testimony was discredited. The public found her untrustworthy, and so did the mostly white jury. George Zimmerman went free.

Untrained for and unaccustomed to the media spotlight, Rachel Jeantel was not code-switching for the white power structure that would be deciding this case. Code-switching is a linguistic term that describes how multilingual people slide easily back and forth between one language or dialect and another, depending upon their context. Black people who speak AAVE do this often, switching between AAVE and Standard English depending on where they are and whom they're talking to. Maya Lewis offers three reasons why she as a Black woman wishes that she could stop code-switching so easily: (1) It requires labor on the part of the "switcher"; (2) it is embedded in assimilation and respectability politics; and (3) it coddles white people by not requiring us to do the work of understanding AAVE.[5]

In the case of Trayvon Martin, the irony is that the white power structure decided that, out of our own lack of knowledge and understanding, Rachel Jeantel was ignorant. It wasn't Rachel who was ignorant—it was us. She was speaking a language fluently that we did not understand, and so we called her dumb. And a young boy's murderer went free because of it. Any good American, any parent, any faithful person who believes in a good and just God should be very, very bothered by this fact.

The first way toward healing—toward redemption and reparations then—is language. This too is what makes language powerful. For everything it can take away, it can also restore and redeem when given license and a listening ear. As Phelps eloquently says, a nation that wants to be just must "take back for itself and its citizens the ability to use language . . . even empower them to tell their own stories, to re-member by remembering."[6] White people must do this work too. We must collectively remember our history in order to put it back together honestly and reunite it with that of the people who have been oppressed by it to find the holistic truth. We must actively remember it in order to stand in the vibrating air as the stories hum around us. We must honor those vibrations for the truth they sing before we can ever hope to be collectively free. We must do the work of repentance and reparations if we want our own souls to heal, to hum with the harmony of wholeness. We are broken for our whitewashed memories, for our refusal to re-member ourselves. Wholeness can only come from the stories we desperately try not to hear.

A big part of that story is the N-word. But that word, though we may have created it, is not ours to own. It's not ours to use. It's a word that we forced into the Black and Brown skin of our siblings with every lash of the whip, every cutting chain. We gave it to them, and now it's theirs, to do with what they will.

Leave it be. That's what a good person would do.

Identity Lost: The History of the N-Word + White Entitlement

Here is one of the grounding acts of language as torture—the monolithic gesture of empire naming every African "Negro" regardless of tribal or national identity. Here is the first step of dehumanization, of the flattening of multitudes of identities into one meaning that was also considered less than ideal. This is a word that is associated with kidnapping people and shipping them to entirely different continents, with ripping children away from their mothers, never to be reunited again. This is a word that is about husbands and wives being torn apart, offered to various "owners." This is a word that has trauma deeply embedded within its consonants and vowels; the very vibrations of the sounds in the air feel evil.

The word has gone through multiple iterations on its journey to the present day. A few months ago, a friend asked my opinion on whether white people should use the N-word. After I explained why I thought white people should *never* use the word, he said something I found very interesting, and something that is aligned with good white racist ideology. He said that Black people should "not feel *entitled* to use the N-word if white people can't" (emphasis mine). He said it's reverse racism, and that Black people should stop blaming white people and not use the word either. But, he added, if they are going to use it as a form of self-directed reclamation, then white people should get to use it too.

Now you're having one of two reactions: either your head is exploding, or you're nodding in enthusiastic agreement. If you're nodding, I hope you're also wearing your "good white racist" ID badge. Because *who's feeling entitled to what now?*

White people like you and me forced this word onto diverse people groups as a method of torture and dehumanization. Like my friend, I wish the word could be erased from our collective consciousness, but to do so would be to perpetuate the emotional torture of Black people by continuing to remove their voice and their ownership over their own histories, not to mention the avoidance of our participation in a very ugly past. As white people who wish to be good, holding onto some sort of twisted ownership of that word—whether by insisting we get to sing along to song lyrics or using it as an ill-advised term of endearment—isn't about equality or our freedom of speech. It's about feeling entitled to something that is ultimately horrific and evil.

It's about being unwilling to put the whip down.

When we pout like five-year-olds, saying, "Well if I can't, then nobody can, including Black people," we've just expanded our tortuous repertoire; we've just added chains to the whip. Here we are, stealing the voice of Black people, appropriating the language of empire, forcing it down their throats and gleefully dancing when they regurgitate it back or getting mad if they spit it out. Worst of all, we deny their healing—and our own. The point of torture is to destroy the voice, to take away language. And here we are, wanting to take away the self-agency of Black people to reclaim a word—or not—that has been used to dehumanize them for centuries.

I may wish the N-word would disappear from our collective consciousness, but that is neither my right nor my privilege to decide. It is solely the work of Black people to reclaim this word as they see fit—whether for its destruction or its resurrection into something new and powerful and profound. This is one of the first steps a good white racist can make toward becoming truly antiracist, toward creating this lovely world we love to lazily banter on about, this dream world where everyone is equal. If we're serious about that, we'll let go of this strange entitlement we have. After all, white people have been going around the globe claiming dominion over everything and everyone, erasing whole identities as easily as we change their names. This can be one thing we give back to the world, the ugly gift of truth that we participated in torture and no longer wish to. Therefore, we humbly submit the grotesque and hideous word to the world, relinquish any claim we've ever tried to stake in it, and step aside to make room for the agency of Black people to self-empower and for once—for one glorious moment—not to have to breathe in air that has been veritably infused with whiteness.

Language and the PC Police:
Where Political Correctness Gets It Wrong

I work hard to use language to uplift my fellow humans, not degrade them. My goal is always, first, to do no harm. For this reason, I am happily politically correct, because honestly, what is often derided as "PC" is just being kind, considerate, and hospitable. I mean, how hard is it, really, to use a person's preferred pronoun, for example? Or to not use gendered language for God? Or to not use the N-word? Does it require thought and intention? Absolutely. Certainly, good white people are capable of this. I mean, *good* people aren't *lazy* people, right?

As scholars and social commentators began to deconstruct language and its power, however, something happened. Not only did we become a more "politically correct" society, but overt racism also went underground. I support the idea of being politically correct, of changing our collective agreement about words and meaning and power. But in many ways, and for many good white racists, that's not what happened. Instead, words changed or left the public lexicon, but ideologies didn't. Ideologies simply became harder to see and root out.

If we are oblivious to the power our whiteness holds, with all its meanings and contexts, we can do massive emotional harm, even when we don't mean to. When a white person uses the N-word, even just in a song, she brings with her into that dynamic all the history of power and meaning that word carries with it. A white person using the word—regardless of its intent—still has a certain sociological meaning that is different than when a Black person uses it. And I remind you: as white people who want to be truly good, we don't get to tell Black people if or how they get to use that word.

My good friend Ben, who is biracial, says this: "When a white person uses the N-word, I immediately have to wonder about my safety when they're around. I have to wonder what they really think of me or race in general. I have to wonder if I'm less valuable to them." I care about Ben, and it breaks my heart that he experiences this in the world. And as a good person, I should care if anyone—not just family and friends—is made to experience this. As a good white racist, as the one who holds the power that is inherent in this word, I should understand the harm it does to my fellow human beings.

But too often, good white racists choose to ignore the power they wield in interactions with people of color when they don't take the power of language seriously. Or they'll practice a politically correct vocabulary while maintaining a racist lexicon of the heart. They may not say out loud that the couple speaking Spanish at the grocery store should learn English, but they'll think it. They may not look at a young Black man and call him a "thug" to his face, but that may be the word that flashes on the inner screen behind their eyes. These thoughts are sometimes so automatic that they go unquestioned and unanalyzed, which makes them dangerous. Truly good people, on the other hand, pay attention, consider the weight of their words (even the ones they don't say out loud). That doesn't mean they'll never make a mistake—but when they do, they'll believe people who tell them that their mistake did harm. They'll listen carefully and try to learn about the context and the layers of meaning they missed.

Truly good people who want to engage in antiracism do the hard work of paying attention.

Action Items

Learn: Look up the racist history of the following common phrases (and maybe eliminate them from your vocabulary): *grandfather clause; peanut gallery; sold down the river;* and *eenie, meenie, miny, moe.*

Think: How have you participated in silencing antiracist voices, removing the voices of BIPOC who are expressing or describing a racial experience? How has language you've used been inherently racist?

Act: The next time you hear a person of color describing a racial experience, don't speak. Listen and learn. The next time a white person uses racist language, speak up, point it out, and refuse to affirm it in any way.

Chapter Five

The Mis-education of America

(Or, *Everything You Know about Being a Good White Racist You Probably Learned in Kindergarten*)

M y girlfriend Donna has three children, two of whom were adopted out of the New Jersey foster care system. Though New Jersey is a pretty diverse place, the town they live in tends to be not so much. Donna's son, Devante, has some developmental issues and can sometimes be disruptive in the classroom. But one day, one of Devante's teachers did a beautiful thing.

She told Donna that she had given herself a test for the day. Every time she was about to correct or call out Devante for a negative behavior, she stopped herself for a hot second, looked around the room, and paid attention to how many other students were engaged in the same exact behavior. The results of her mini-experiment were shocking and fruitful. More often than not, at least three or four other kids in the class were doing the exact same thing. Devante was just being a normal kid, squirming and being silly.

Of course, for a teacher, maintaining control in a classroom is imperative for learning. But we've learned from previous chapters about how implicit bias works, about how black is associated with bad things and white with good things, and about how people of color have essentially been erased from positions of authority in the education system. Combine that with the colonialist mindset of empire, in which the narrative is controlled by the victors, force-feed that into the forming gelatinous globs that are the

71

developing brains of children, and you have the perfect system for maintaining the status quo—a veritable factory line of good white racists who will be so ingrained with the white supremacist narrative that they will rarely, if ever, question it. The education system is one of the primary ways in which our racist society is maintained. It's time now to put our thinking caps on, grab our juice boxes and crackers, and have a good hard look at how our own educations may have made us good white racists without our even knowing it. Even more shocking is that it may have been good people who thought they were being truly antiracist who did the most harm.

Power Differentials and Whiteness

Though it's rarely spoken about, white people are hyperaware of the power dynamic we bring to any interaction with people of color. Our professed color blindness and our intense attempts not to do or say anything that might be considered racist is really just an awkward attempt to ignore the truth of the power we bring to these relationships. We all know it's there—and it makes most white people crazy uncomfortable. Place a white person—even an antiracist one (perhaps *especially* an antiracist one)—into an *actual* position of power and authority over a member of the BIPOC community (such as a teacher), and suddenly the power dynamic folds in on itself, reinstates its power, and reinforces stereotypes and racist narratives—and not for lack of good intentions. In fact, it's *because* of good intentions. Brian M. McCadden claims that when a white person holds authority over a member of the BIPOC community, a deep sense of fear, dread, and anxiety arises in the white person and causes even well-intentioned educators to do greater harm by trying to help more.

In his essay titled "Why Is Michael Always Timed Out," McCadden brilliantly breaks down the way this power dynamic plays out—and it's not because of a teacher who is intentionally racist. Rather, it's because of a teacher who has been so infiltrated with the narrative of the white empire that she cannot see how her good work and highest intentions actually do great harm, not just to Michael and the other Black children in her care, but also to the white children in her class, who absorb the racist narrative like tiny little sponges, becoming embedded with the same seed of whiteness, gulping down the narrative like hungry birds being fed in the nest. And nobody notices. Whiteness is, after all, that invisible ocean.

And worst of all? Even if everyone noticed, they might not choose to change a thing, because what Mrs. Hooper the good white racist teacher does so well is to teach whiteness to her students—especially to her students of color. Her goal, even if she wouldn't call it by name, is to teach her students how to obediently swim in that ocean called white empire.

McCadden's essay is an analysis of time he spent observing a highly successful kindergarten teacher in a fairly progressive, liberal North Carolina town. Primarily white, with a small BIPOC community, the town was known for its exceptional schools; in such a school system, Mrs. Hooper stood out as a kindergarten teacher among kindergarten teachers. Black and white parents alike sought her out, specifically requesting her for their children, because she was so successful at preparing her students for the rest of their academic careers.

During his observations, however, McCadden noticed that Black children—especially boys—were often more harshly disciplined than white boys for similar behavior. Yet McCadden does not claim that Mrs. Hooper is a racist. In fact, Mrs. Hooper was a champion for racial equality in the school, regularly challenging the school board to be more inclusive in its curriculum and progressive in its racial leadership. Still, despite her antiracist actions and her deep desire to serve *all* her students, Mrs. Hooper was a tool for the white empire.

First, as McCadden points out, Mrs. Hooper employs a teacher-centric modality in the classroom—an ethos that revolves around responding to the teacher's authority as success. This is a factory-line template to American education—the idea that the system as a whole is designed to churn out well-behaved workers equipped to use their basic knowledge to serve first and foremost "the orga-nization"—whether that's the education system in which they'll spend the next twelve or so years, the company they'll work for later, or the status quo of the white empire.

Second, McCadden identifies among white educators a dearth of awareness and appreciation of cultures other than whiteness. This leads to multiple misunderstandings on several levels and involves the coded language of whiteness to privilege white students. But because much of the white teacher's language is coded for whiteness, Black children are at a disadvantage and may not understand the teacher's instructions or reprimands. Their so-called bad behavior is compounded, which results in more negative attention. McCadden uses the following example of culturally coded language: a white child would understand that the question "Is that where the scissors belong?" really means, "Put the scissors on the shelf," while a child who had not been raised with this type of coded language might receive the question as a literal one, with several possible answers. His response would be considered cheeky at best; at worst, it would reinforce a "problem child" label. The white teacher would never notice that this was a cultural miscommunication rather than a behavioral issue, because whiteness is the standard, the norm against which all are to conform. The fact that a child might not understand this coded question—indeed, the fact that it is coded at all—would be completely off Mrs. Hooper's peda-gogical radar.[1]

Also at play here is the constructed narrative among white people that Black children are harder to control or that they do not receive discipline at home. Called "deficit ideology," this nar-rative leads the good white racist teacher—who genuinely wants her students to succeed in the world of whiteness—to pay extra attention to Black students, often in the form of harsher disci-pline, out of a belief that they require more attention than white kids in order to succeed in the world.

In his analysis, McCadden seems to be afraid to call Mrs. Hooper a racist. I'm not afraid to do so, however, because her racism has nothing to do with her intentions, her desire to help her students of color succeed, or her goodness. Rather, her racism is the embedded invisible empire at work, the pride she takes in preparing her students to meet the demands of empire, and the fact that, even if she were aware of how her racism is at play, reality would not prompt her to dismantle it. The reality of our culture states that what she does is in the best interest of her students—all of them. And that means preparing them to be good little cogs in the wheel of the white empire.

But in fact, when she reprimands her students who are Black more often than she does her white ones—even if she does so lovingly—she perpetuates the racist stereotype that inherent in Blackness is a deficit. Not because her reprimand is unwarranted. No one is saying that Black kids are angels who don't need discipline. But when children who are white and engaged in the same behavior get gentle, almost joking reprimands, and when they can understand her coded corrections more easily than Black children, the white children in the room notice. They notice, and they begin to internalize the construct of whiteness as good and Blackness as not so much. White students will grow up to be good white racists themselves, believing somewhere deep in their brains that children of color need extra help, extra handling, and extra discipline, because we need to prepare them for the empire of whiteness, and they simply just don't measure up.

White Reformers: The History of Educating for Whiteness

This framework is not unprecedented in history. Since the American education system came into being and the need to educate both Native American and African American children became obvious in the 1800s, there have been well-intentioned—and hella racist—white people who were ready to answer the call. And when I say "hella racist," I am again not talking about intentions or even goodness. These people had the *best* of intentions, and probably even suffered the wrath of their fellow white people—the people you might think of as the pointy-hood-wearing *real* racists—for even attempting to participate in the uplift of these BIPOC communities. But the truth is, they came to their endeavors with highly racialized thinking and held beliefs about race that were rooted in false ideas of biological ability. They saw race as a way to biologically distinguish between groups of people and then placed these groups into a racial hierarchy based on biological ability, with whiteness at the top of the pyramid.[2] The goal was assimilation, and the method was the removal of culture whenever possible. In the case of people whose skin tone kept them from ever fully assimilating into whiteness, the goal was to keep them docile and compliant.

Because these reformers saw themselves and their whiteness as the models for success and goodness—and perpetually superior to the BIPOC communities they claimed to serve—they believed that they could help their students fit into and find success within the white empire (albeit to a lesser degree than any white student). This was their idea of compassion—recognizing that these children would never be white, but at least they could pretend to be, and that would be best for everyone involved. When it came to indigenous populations, the reformers hoped that after a few generations of enculturation, First Nations people might eventually disappear completely as a distinct racial group and merge entirely with whites.[3] No such hope existed for Black students, however, though the reformers hoped that proper schooling would help them become better Americans, make them more productive, and allow them to maneuver within the white empire, if not with outright success then at least with the basic creature comforts. This was good white racist thinking—it maintained the racial hierarchy through institutional means.

These narratives are still at play today in our school systems, even with all our diversity programming and political correctness. Whiteness still controls the dominant narrative, and paramount to that narrative is the idea of being *nice*. Above all else, good white racists are obsessed with being *nice*. After all, everything you ever needed to know about being nice—about being a good white racist—you probably learned in kindergarten.

Nice 'n' White: The Colonization of Little White Minds

I remember well the way the Thanksgiving story was taught to me in school. Friendly pilgrims and happy Indians shared a meal together, and the great American tradition was born. Oh, and the Indians had to teach those silly pilgrims how to plant corn. We made Indian headdresses out of Elmer's glue and construction paper, but we never heard mention of blankets covered in smallpox, of the rape and pillaging of Native tribes, or of the way Native Americans are not allowed to own their own land. Instead, the story is whitewashed and sanitized so that America—and by proxy, Americans—can look good. Everyone in the story is always *super nice*. School taught us to be *nice*. *Niceness* is a key component of good white racism. And American schools are full of it.

Niceness is what makes white people sympathetic about the harm done to BIPOC communities because of racism, but it's also what keeps them from doing anything about it. Being nice means you don't upset the status quo. Being nice requires a complicit nature, one that does not disrupt or question or boldly point out errors in logic. Ultimately, niceness is about tiptoeing around the white American male and all *his* comfort levels, his sense of entitlement, and his right to maintain his liberty at the cost of justice for all. It's about helping white women to toe the feminine line, to ensure the world knows of her goodness, her righteousness, of all the ways she lives up to some weird, yoga-pants-wearing version of the Proverbs 31 woman. Niceness tells us to just shut up about race already, because Oprah is rich and therefore everything's *fine*.

Niceness and the deficit ideology go hand in hand, in that they allow white people to feel good about ourselves for the help we give to those we perceive as less than us. It's a tool that many American teachers use in their attempts at multicultural education, in which they emphasize not the structural power differentials that marginalized communities experience (such as the criminalization of poverty or the bias of the justice system) but rather accessibility and diverse learning styles, making sure that each child has access to needed services and teaching methods.

These are important, but they are only the beginning steps to dismantling the white empire, and our self-satisfaction with intermittently providing them leaves us sorely lacking when it comes to actually being effective antiracists.

The theory of interest convergence states that people believe in what benefits them and that the majority group will tolerate and/or pursue advances for racial justice only when there is a perception of benefit.[4] In education, this usually manifests as some sort of diversity or multicultural curriculum implemented as a response to a racial crisis. But the curriculum is both formed and administered within the construct of whiteness, and so ultimately it is whiteness these programs serve. The programs are based in promoting sameness rather than affirming difference and are often about mitigating white discomfort that arises because of a racial event. Students celebrate Black History Month, and a diversity box gets checked off. Everyone feels warm and fuzzy listening to the pretty parts of Martin Luther King Jr.'s *I Have a Dream* speech, because nothing in that part of the speech actually depicts white power or its deconstruction. We ignore the part where he calls out America for defaulting on its promise, we disregard his disdain for gradualism, we forget the part where he said we'd all be in for a rude awakening if things didn't change. We go straight to the part where white people look good, because they are holding hands with Black people.

Because these programs, and the educators who administer them, believe and participate in white *niceness*, the one thing that could actually disrupt and dismantle the white empire is never discussed: power differentials. Wanting the white empire to stay invisible, we don't teach about the ways structural injustice occurs every day in our courts or economies, in our government or our workplaces. Teaching about these things would make them visible and more likely to be dismantled. Instead, teachers consider "different styles and levels of learning"; classrooms hold holiday feasts in which children bring in the cherished dishes of their culture; maybe, somewhere, a rogue teacher will mention that perhaps Christopher Columbus wasn't such a nice guy, after all. But nobody talks about white power, and so therefore, no one ever deconstructs it. Because nothing will make white people more uncomfortable than to point out the truth of our power.

I mean, that just wouldn't be *nice*.

One of the ways this niceness is performed in the school system is the way we administer multicultural programs only in schools that have a large diversity of children. Because, you know, schools that have mostly white kids in them don't really need to learn diversity awareness. Because the world isn't diverse or anything.

This is a perfect example of interest convergence theory; there isn't a need for multicultural awareness until there is some sort of multicultural crisis. The status quo is fine as long as it's not disrupted by racialized events. When a Starbucks employee calls the police on some Black men just existing, or a convenience store clerk tells two customers, "Go back to where you come from," whiteness jumps into multicultural overdrive as a way to paternalistically pat everyone on the head. We program and train and promote the appropriate lexicon, but we don't actually do anything that's much more than self-congratulatory diversity efforts. Because whiteness needs to be considered both compassionate and responsive (and of course totally not racist), we perform lip service to multicultural training and curricula but don't actually ever implement any real antiracist change—such as disrupting the white power differential.

In the case of the Starbucks incident—and all the other "while Black" incidents that pepper the interwebz with examples of white people being racist—the only way institutional white power would begin to be dismantled is if the agents of the state (in this case the police) began to behave differently. If police began to ticket white people for placing false or unnecessary calls to the police, for example, Black people might finally be safe to just be. If police were better trained to respond appropriately when they do answer those calls—by focusing on the person who made the false call rather than automatically arresting the person of color—then the first tiny thread of institutional racism might be pulled, and perhaps then, the whole system might start to unravel.

White Power and *Huckleberry Finn*

A practical example of this is what happens in a classroom when a curriculum includes books such as *Huckleberry Finn*, a work that uses the N-word over 200 times. There are so many dynamics to consider here, the most important being the impact this has on Black students, especially those in predominantly white classrooms led by white teachers. I'm torn on whether the book should be taught. As a writer, I'm aware of both the importance of the literary canon and its racialized and gendered exclusivity (which I find obnoxious, at best). I don't like censorship, and the brutal truth of the book can do a lot to enlighten students about our not-so-awesome American past. But harm is harm, and it's important to not just be aware of that, but to take responsibility for that and to do something about it. Ultimately, I think it should be left up to Black educators to decide whether the book should be taught as written, and how.

That said, for the bravest of teachers (and hopefully, well trained and antiracist), an exploration of this text could be part of a new way to educate children for the purpose of deconstructing whiteness and leveling power differentials, rather than reiterating them. Imagine if a teacher were to teach *Huckleberry Finn* alongside works by BIPOC authors such as Frederick Douglass to demonstrate power dynamics, to humanize those who have been dehumanized by the power of language, to empower those who have been left out of canons, silenced and marginalized. Imagine if white teachers openly discussed and taught students about the history of the N-word, about its power and its ownership and why it is a word that white people should never use. Imagine if white teachers helped their white students actually *see* whiteness rather than get lost in it and helped them understand the way it operates in literature, in the classroom, and in the world.

Perhaps if white teachers could use their explicit authority in this way to deconstruct whiteness—to make visible what has been to white people invisible and to BIPOC communities a figurative—and at times, very literal—noose around their necks, perhaps then we might finally have a chance at a future without racism.

White Empire, Black Bodies, and School

Before we close the chapter on education and the white empire, we have to discuss another bizarre and harmful phenomenon that takes place in classrooms and main offices in schools around the country: children's bodies policed for, well, basically existing.

To examine this issue well, we must consider something we haven't yet discussed: the white male ownership of space. This concept is at the crux of much of what props up and supports the white patriarchy, and it's centered on the idea that white men rule any space in which they move, and by proxy, also own everything in it. As a result, everyone else—women and BIPOC communities—needs to make themselves smaller in those spaces, to conform our bodies and our behavior to keep the white men happy. Male ownership of space is what leads to catcalling and harassment of women in public spaces. Entitlement is assumed. Men can say whatever they want to the women who move through "their" space.

White ownership of space is also a thing, and when members of the BIPOC community move through white spaces, the assumed requirement by whiteness is conformity to white norms. This includes everything from culturally approved behavior, dress, and speech to compliance with white beauty standards. And as a white woman, let me tell you that white beauty standards are no cakewalk. You have to be stick thin until you're supposed to be curvy. You're supposed to have bangs until you cut them, then they're suddenly out of style. Your skin has to be clear, and your belly may not roll, and basically anything that goes along with being a normal female—like thick thighs or (God forbid) a wrinkle or a gray hair—is basically, somehow, a flaw. Because ultimately, your body is meant primarily for the enjoyment of and consumption by men.

Needless to say, Black women have it even harder, between skin tones that don't match so-called "nude" products from Band-Aids to pantyhose to makeup, facial features that are undervalued for their rich fullness, and hair that must be straightened into an unnatural state. The patriarchal beauty standards that have been force-fed to white women, to which we have molded and shaped ourselves to the best of our abilities, may seem completely unattainable for BIPOC bodies. And one of the first places bodies are judged and scrutinized is in school.

Like our good white racist teachers with nice intentions, the white empire's educational system works to prepare children to conform to its white norms, to "succeed" in a white world. In fact, studies clearly show that Black students are more likely to receive "criminalized discipline"—the introduction of police into a situation, for example—while white students are more likely to receive "medicalized discipline" (a diagnosis of and the subsequent adjustments that go with ADHD, for example).[5] But just as this goal causes Black children to be punished more harshly, their bodies are also scrutinized more closely—and they're often set up to fail. Girls in general are subjected to ridiculous dress codes solely because boys may be "distracted" by their body parts, such as shoulders, knees, and collarbones—you know, the usual sexy parts. Black children, however, are subject to additional norms about what constitutes "neatness"—because the hair that naturally grows out of their heads doesn't cut it, unless it is pulled and straightened and changed to conform to whiteness—the white male patriarchal view of what is beautiful. Google "school suspension" and "braids," for example, and you'll find a plethora of instances in which young girls have had their educations interrupted for wearing their hair in braids, or for wearing extensions that make caring for their hair easier. (Happily, you might also find news about the state of California's most recent legislation banning discrimination for natural or protective hairstyles—but consider the fact that *it took a law to make this okay*.) Meanwhile, these girls could wear their hair in its natural state, and it still won't be acceptable—apparently, only hair that is straightened (i.e., more like white hair) makes the grade.

Boys who are members of the BIPOC community are not excused from this rule either. Hair that is natural, cut into a design, braided, or in dreads is considered a "distraction." And the result? These children's educations are disrupted. They are removed from the classroom and sent home from school, their learning interrupted all because they have failed to exist in space according to a white norm.

Practically from its inception, the education system in the United States has been an invisible cog in the wheel of structural racism, helping to keep systemic injustice hidden while, at the same time, being an active participant in it, both implicitly and explicitly. Not only does it continue to harm children of color, but it churns out oblivious good white racists at an alarming rate who believe many of the false narratives and myths that whiteness perpetrates. As we turn to chapter 6, let's begin to unpack some of the most common stories we good white racists love to tell ourselves.

Action Items

Learn: Review your school system's teaching and administrative staff. Can you find diversity there? Also, review the curriculum—are BIPOC voices included?

Think: Think back to your own education. Can you spot the racist narratives? What assumptions have you built around them?

Act: Pay attention to what the children in your life are learning in school. Confront racist narratives and provide alternatives.

Chapter Six

Justifying Ourselves

(Or, *"But Black People Owned Slaves!"*)

The justifications are everywhere. They pop up in conversations I have with friends and in my social media feed by way of poorly designed memes. They are contained in the apathetic shrugs of family members; they are yelled from the veiny-throated, apoplectic conspiracy theorists on right-wing talk shows. Almost anywhere you turn, you can find someone giving you a reason why it's totally okay to deny that racism exists, to avoid acknowledging our own racist behavior, and to pretend everything's fine.

The only thing, though, is that it's not.

When we actually apply some functioning brain matter to the situation (not to mention some empathy and basic human decency), and when we are willing to understand the truth of paradox and hierarchy and human complexity, we can understand that racial truth in America is far more intricate and nuanced than any jibe a simple meme or screaming pundit can offer—and that's on either side of the aisle. It's about people and systems, and about many things being true at once, and while we can certainly twist the truth to make ourselves feel better and get ourselves off the proverbial hook, the truth of the matter is that if we are truly good people, we won't want to get off the hook if it means people are suffering. If we are *truly* good, we will do the hard work of deconstructing these paradoxical truths, untangling the

85

complexity, and changing the embedded structures that are causing harm. For those of us who claim to follow Jesus, I believe this becomes even more important, because our faith is one of deep self-reflection and, ultimately, repentance.

While you go ahead and ruminate on that, I will go ahead and break down some of the most popular justifications I've heard people use to explain why everything's fine and there's no need to change the status quo because America is totally not a racist country.

"But Black People Owned Slaves!"

Any time a conversation comes up around the topic of slavery and the possibility that perhaps reparations should be made for the chattel slavery that Black people endured over generations in this country, inevitably someone's eyebrows go high, eyes go wide, and hands gesticulate as they exclaim, "But Black people owned slaves too!" And it's true. Not only did Black people own slaves, but they sold slaves and profited from the slave trade as well.

Let's get the first, most obvious thing out of the way first: *that doesn't make it right.* I mean, do I really even need to say this? Blackness does not automatically absolve one of the potential for assholey-ness. Assholey-ness is a transracial phenomenon. The fact that Black people owned their fellow human beings and profited from the legal trade of chattel slavery should never be a justification that things were okay then or are okay now. At best, it's a superficial and lazy explanation; at worst, it's practically almost saying, "Black people owned slaves, and I would too if I had the chance and a plantation." In other words, it's gross.

But let's dig a little deeper. Certainly, and just like almost every other society on earth, African tribes fought with one another, kidnapped one another, and enslaved one another. But it was the *white empire* that created a market for human chattel. It was a supply and demand issue, and make no mistake about it: the product was human lives, and it was the white empire that supplied the demand. The Africans who traded and profited from their fellow Africans don't get off the hook; but they can neither be held responsible for hundreds of years of an evil industry nor used as justification for our racist systems still in place today.

So yes, it's true that Black people in America owned slaves. However, 42 percent of Black slaveholders owned just one—most likely, these were family members, such as spouses or children, they purchased in order to remove them from the auction block permanently.[1] Black people who owned more than one slave were often men who had purchased their wives and neglected to officially emancipate them, resulting in their children automatically being born into "slavery." Black slave owners who actually participated in the for-profit slave trade were few and far between and definitely in the wrong, but they were no more in the wrong than the hundreds of thousands of slave owners who were white. Of all the slave owners in America, less than 1 percent were Black. The fact that they existed does not justify slavery, nor does it excuse or make up for the generations of disadvantage that descendants of slaves have endured since the emancipation.

"The Irish Were Slaves Too!" (And the Perennial Favorite: "Not MY Ancestors!")

Let's be clear: Were the Irish colonized by the British and treated abysmally by them? Hell, yes. Do the Irish have a long history of being trampled on, invaded, and marginalized in their own homeland? Of being colonized and Anglicized, with their language and culture stolen and erased? Absolutely. Were they kidnapped from their beloved green isle, shackled and handcuffed, stuffed onto shelves side by side, shoulder to shoulder in tiny little compartments, shipped across the Atlantic, then sold when they arrived on an American auction block to the highest bidder for a lifetime of torture, subsistence, and hard labor?

No. No they were not.

There is no doubt that indentured servitude sucked. The British absolutely screwed up Ireland just like they screwed up practically every other continent they and their fellow imperialists touched. (I'm looking at you, Portugal, Spain, and the Netherlands). Trust me when I tell you that my Irish heritage allows me no great love for Great Britain and its imperial ways, and the pain and suffering in Ireland as a result of its invaders is still apparent today; it still flares up in the pubs and the streets on both sides of the pond. I've been in enough Irish bars in the Bronx to know.

But indentured servitude was not slavery. It was an agreement you (or your parents) entered into willingly, a contract you signed for passage to the Americas. Those contracts eventually expired, so there was an end in sight, and your eventual freedom was assured. While it's true that many indentured servants died before their contracts expired, many more found freedom and were able then to assimilate into society by virtue of their skin color and begin their upward mobilization, which in turn ensured their descendants even more success in the land of the free and the home of the brave. Though the Irish did, indeed, experience discrimination, it was mostly about their brogue; once they lost the lilt to their words (an accent I must say I am quite partial to and that can make me go weak in the knees to this day), they could slide into the invisible comfort of whiteness. If this did not happen for first-generation Irish, it most definitely happened in subsequent generations. Unlike Black and Brown people, the Irish (and other light-skinned immigrant groups) were able to assimilate into whiteness relatively quickly and easily, and as a result, they did not suffer generations of systemic oppression, economic or otherwise.

Similar to this argument is the common "*My* ancestors never owned slaves!" debate, often promoted by those who are the descendants of, if not the Irish, more recent immigrants. "My ancestors were still living in thatched-roof huts in some quaint European village with fairies and elves" is what these protests of innocence seem to be saying. The very opulence and opportunity that sparkles in the American identity like the stars in our flag and that beckoned your ancestors to its shine was built with the blood, sweat, and tears of enslaved human beings with beautiful, Black skin. There is no getting around the fact that we simply don't know how the American experiment would have fared if not for an economy imbued with and dependent upon the strong backs of enslaved African men and women. It's very possible that we owe Africa our very existence for all we have taken from it in resources, both material and especially human.

Regardless of when your family arrived here, if you identify as white, then at some point you and your ancestors slipped on the cloak of the white empire and have moved through its privileged systems ever since. If you have not been subject to "separate but ~~not really~~ equal," redlining, or inequitable justice systems based on the color of your skin, then you have moved through the empire as one assigned privilege. In that case, it makes no difference that your people never owned slaves. There's still a spot on the whip handle with your name on it.

"Oprah's Rich and Obama Was President, So Everything's Fine"

White people often point to people like Oprah Winfrey and Barack Obama as proof that we're living in a "postracial" society—whatever the hell that is. Talk about sticking your head in the sand. *Just let me keep insisting that racism isn't a thing anymore over the chants of these Black Lives Matter protesters over here.* Just because some Black people have been wildly successful does not absolve America of our historical cruelty and the sin of slavery or mean that the BIPOC community in general is doing just fine.

BIPOC communities have been denied the accumulation of wealth for generations. They are not fine. Through a number of structural obstacles—such as redlining, subpar education and services, and inequitable job opportunities—people of color have been kept at an economic disadvantage since they first stepped foot on our shores. And when I say disadvantage, I'm talking about a *huge* one: for example, the median wealth of Black families in the United States in 2016 was $13,460, compared to $142,180 for white families.[2] Compounding this problem is that Black families are more likely to experience a financial crisis that requires wealth they don't have—which puts them further into debt. Blacks still experience far more systemic obstacles to wealth creation. Their debt costs more due to higher interest rates; they have limited access to wealth-creating programs such as retirement plans because of historic discrimination in the jobs that provide them, and they have been subject to redlining and discriminatory mortgage practices, leading to a lower valuation of their properties.[3] The numbers make this clear.

This is what it means to have white privilege. Privilege doesn't mean that we haven't worked hard for what we have, or that our lives have not had difficulties. When someone says you have privilege, they are not saying that you hate Black people and purposefully try to keep them down. But one of its meanings is that as white people, we did not experience the same kinds of systemic obstacles to economic prosperity that BIPOC have, and neither did our ancestors. So even if you haven't had it easy, chances are you've still had it easier than the Black person sitting next to you.

"But Black-on-Black Crime!"

Let's start here: it's not a thing.

Do Black people hurt other Black people? Absolutely. Does that happen just because they're Black? Not exactly.

Here's one important point: this loaded term, "Black-on-Black crime," doesn't just mean that Black people are perpetrating crimes. That's the narrative that people who tout this story love to embed in our brains—that there is some sort of inherent criminality present in Black people that makes "Black-on-Black" crime more prominent.

Like so many race-related narratives, the concept of Black-on-Black crime is an oversimplified distraction intended to keep us good white racists from really understanding the complexities of poverty, race, and the white empire. "Black-on-Black crime" is intended to let us think we have nothing to do with it—that it's not our fault that Black people can't help but destroy themselves, and therefore, it's okay for police to "control" them with force. This is an example of the "savage construct" we'll discuss at length later in this chapter. In reality, though? It's dehumanizing and flat out wrong.

"Black-on-Black" crime happens not because Black people want to hurt other Black people or are naturally prone to criminal behavior, but because—just like "white-on-white" crime—violence most often happens among people who know each other. As my friend and former police officer Lisa Boeving-Learned pointed out in a private email exchange, "It's the dark side of humanity. Most criminals don't travel far from where they live to commit crime." Lisa also makes a salient point: that the overpolicing of Black neighborhoods, the criminalization of poverty, and the stereotypes that promote assumptions that all Black people are criminals lead to skewed statistics that appear to prove the point but in actuality don't tell a complete truth. Part of that truth is that Black people are the *victims* of crime more often than white people. In fact, you know those scary Black teenage boys you love to be afraid of because they're wearing hoodies while shopping for Skittles? They—yes, they—are more likely to be *victims* of violent crime than white people are.[4] This doesn't even count the crimes committed against young Black bodies by the police (we'll get to that in later chapters).

"Talking about Race Is Racist"

At the beginning of Black History Month this past February, I was suddenly inspired to create a meme for social media that listed ten ways white people can celebrate Black History Month. I was surprised at how quickly it started spreading, and the comments on my Instagram account started going crazy. Aside from the usual, completely unoriginal objections, there was, of course, the expected "woke" white woman who is convinced she's got this race thing all worked out, because she "once took a class on race that was taught by a Black man." She decided to educate me.

"We all need to stop apologizing for this particular social construct and see our similarities!" she exclaimed. "We're all the same y'all but we will never be treated the same if we keep pointing out our differences."

Here is a good white racist at work, reinforcing empire and, at the same time, being used by empire to propagate racist systems in which she'd like to think she played no part. "No," I responded. "That is a perspective that originates in and perpetuates privilege."

"Interesting," she replied. "I learned a lot about race from a racial studies class, taught by a Black man. Race was made up by us and we keep it going—you know that, right? It's a social construct (fact, not my opinion). My perspective actually removes racism eventually. Yours perpetuates it."

She thinks she's participating in true antiracism here, but in actuality, she is participating in the social construct of whiteness that insists on maintaining the status quo. The status quo is rarely equivalent to fairness, equity, or equal accessibility and utilization of resources. It's about maintaining current power structures, and it becomes destabilized anytime someone points out its inequities. By insisting that talking about racism perpetuates racism, and attempting to silence me and stop me from pointing out racism and/or participating in racial uplift, she is solidly on the side of the white empire, happily raising her hand and saying, "Pick me! Pick me! I'll be your tool today."

I confirmed that race is absolutely a social construct, but it is one so embedded in our collective psyches that it creates severe and very real consequences for the BIPOC community, and also for the white people who participate in and benefit from white privilege. I told her that it is a social construct that has been institutionalized and systemized to arbitrarily privilege one group over all the others. That's why a perspective that says, "If we stop talking about it, it will go away," doesn't work; it simply maintains the status quo, which benefits whiteness. In order for racism to cease to exist, we must do the work of breaking down the systems and institutions that perpetuate it. And we can't do that without talking about it. Talking about it, though, is only the beginning.

Most white people simply don't like to talk about race, and we tell ourselves it's because it perpetuates racism. But really it's because we've been raised to believe that our whiteness is invisible, and racialized conversations throw a spotlight on that which we'd like to keep hidden.

"I Don't See Race—I'm Color-blind"

I have a confession to make. When I thought about this particular comment that's so popular with good white racists, I realized that when I think about my good friends of color, rarely is my first thought, "OMG, they are *so* Black!" (or Filipino, or Puerto Rican, or whatever). For a hot second, this made me want to say something along the lines of, "Gee, I don't even think of them as Black. I must be color-blind." Luckily, I was alone in the room at the time—and I'm happy to report that this thought didn't even get so far that it fell out of my mouth. I checked myself long enough to figure out what I really meant by that, and that's when I realized how powerful true love actually is. I love these people, and since I love them, we are fully embodied to each other. Let me explain.

We are all a color of some sort. Some people are Black, or Brown, or vaguely tan. Some of us, like me, are so white that we're tinted blue for the veins you can practically see through our skin (thank you, Irish heritage). In our racialized world, our colors go ahead of us wherever we go. They enter the room first, carrying all their baggage with them. They carry the cultural and sociological baggage of what our colors mean to the greater society at large, and they carry with them our personal racialized experiences. They carry our coded language and ways of being and moving in space. They are the first things other people see about us, and that can sometimes become either a barrier or an entryway into relationship.

Think about it this way for a moment, and imagine two people facing each other, their colors between them like opaque representatives of their true selves. They construct meaning about each other, themselves, and the possibilities of relationship with each other based on these representations and the meanings associated with them. But as their friendship grows, as they move into relationship with each other, they step into that shaded representation of themselves—they embody it, they animate it with their personalities, their desires, the things that make them laugh. It is no longer the first or only thing they see about each other—but it is inherently them. The deeper I fall in love with my friends, whatever their color, the more fully embodied we are to each other, and the more deeply we can experience each other—our laughter, our intimate conversations, our deep empathy, the protectiveness we feel for each other, our apologies. Our Blackness and whiteness don't fall away or disappear but rather become an embodied, storied part of our caring and love for each other, and they are always seen and always loved because they are a part of us. We are not blind to each other's color; we are whole to it.

Now, all of what I just said right there? That's a totally white way of seeing the situation.

That doesn't mean it's bad, or that my friends in the BIPOC community don't agree to some extent. It just means it's privileged. I love my friends of color, and even though all of the above is deeply true, the *other* thing that is true is that I love them enough—usually—to be hyperaware of how my whiteness may operate in our dynamic, because the last thing I want to do is harm these people I love. I mean, I can be thoughtless enough just being *me*, forget about me with all my capital-W Whiteness.

I *think* and I *hope* that my closest friends who are of color know my heart, will call me out on any shit my whiteness tries to pull, and still love me for it. I *hope* that they can fully embody their own identity around me. But I also know that probably they can't. Recently I was at a conference, and most of the people I was hanging out with were women of color. One night, though, they decided they wanted to have a BIPOC-only dinner. I know that it's important for people of color to have their own spaces—places where whiteness will not even need to be a factor.

But still.

I felt left out. I got a little nervous that I'd be eating dinner alone. (I didn't. I found a bunch of nice white people to eat dinner with, and we had a great time.) But at the same time, I was happy that they did that—that they created space for themselves, because after a few days in an *Oh-my-God-this-is-a-totally-white-space*, they needed to practice some serious self-care. If I am going to *really* love my friends of color, I have to recognize that our respective colors—and the power dynamics that go with them—mean that sometimes people of color just need a space of their own. We get to love them on their way to those sacred places. And on the off chance that I am ever actually invited into those spaces, my mantra forever will be: *Kerry, don't be an asshole.*

But that's not how good white racists think when they say they are color-blind. Usually, what they *really* mean is that they don't want to acknowledge the fact that race exists, that there is a power dynamic at play, and that there's some work they might need to do to dismantle it. If you're saying you're color-blind, that tells me you're not interested in real relationship with people of color, because to claim you don't see their racial identity is to obliviate their embodied experience, the way they live and move through the world. You cannot holistically see them as people with storied experiences, both racialized and not. Your colors—theirs and yours—will always just be smoky shadow representatives of your true selves, relating only on the surface, with all the racial dynamics in play.

Also, when you claim you don't see color, you're basically lying. Of course you see color—yours and theirs. And it probably makes you crazy uncomfortable. So you'd rather pretend not to see it, because then you won't have to acknowledge the way their racial identity and your privilege operate in the world. This is a denial of extravagant proportions that is intended not for the betterment of people of color, but to keep white people feeling comfortable and righteous.

"But You're Not Like the Rest of Them"

Okay, so this one isn't exactly a justification as much as an exercise in being ridiculously obtuse. And I confess, I'm going to break my own rule here and sort of speak for the BIPOC community, in that I will be retelling stories I've heard far too many times from my friends.

I am a martial artist, and one of my trainers, Jacquim, is both Black and a Muslim. I've been training with him for years, and we've both seen people come and go through the MMA class he teaches. Many times these people will send us friend requests on Facebook, which is where we both discover what they really think. Occasionally, Jacquim and I talk about what we see there. He tells me about conversations he has with people in which he confronts them about their Islamophobia (which often intersects with rabid racism) and says to them, "You know, when you say those things, you're talking about *me*." More often than not, they just shrug their shoulders and say, "But you're different."

But the thing is, he's not. He's just a person, going about his business, not doing a damn thing to anybody (until he decides you're going to be the test dummy he demonstrates a jiu jitsu move on in class—he is not very likable in those moments, but trust me when I say you're in no position to say so at the time). And he's exactly like millions of other Black Muslims in the world who go about their day not doing a damn thing to anybody.

But something in the collective consciousness of the white empire has latched on to a very specific idea of what a Muslim looks like, acts like, and behaves like in everyday life, and it's something more akin to a radicalized monster intent on waging jihad to destroy America. Regardless of how many peace-loving, kind, and caring Muslims we happen to meet, we're convinced that Muslims are personified evil running around with machetes and decapitated heads in baskets, as Fox News would have us believe. Should we happen to actually enter into relationship with a person we genuinely like and then discover "Holy crap! They're *Muslim!*" rather than change our idea of Islam and Muslims in general, we decide that this totally normal, interesting, and kind person must be the exception.

That makes me wonder: Who is the one who has actually been radicalized here?

The fact is that sociopaths come in all colors, and if you run the numbers (go ahead—I'll wait) you'll discover that since 1982, white men have murdered 588 of the 888 victims killed in mass shootings in the United States.[5] At this moment, you might find yourself saying, "But not all white people are mass murderers!" And that's exactly the point. One sociopath doth not for a population speak.

Muslim Americans are just as concerned as other Americans about extremist terrorism, with 82 percent of them claiming to be "very concerned," compared to 83 percent of the general public. In other words, Muslims are people who get scared too. And despite the horrific realities of 9/11, Muslim Americans are more likely than the general American public to say that killing innocent civilians is never okay in the pursuit of a political, social, or religious cause.[6] This goes to show that our stereotypical image of the rabid Islamic radical is way off base from reality.

Another way the whole "But you're not like the rest" mindset plays out is in a strange sort of debate when a member of the BIPOC community calls out a white person for their racism. My friend Nate, who is of Japanese descent, tells me that white people often tell him that *other* Asian people aren't upset by what they say, so he shouldn't be either.

Let's unpack that.

First of all, no community is a monolith of belief systems. While there are of course similarities in thought and beliefs, communities are made up of individuals. My friend Nate does not represent Asian people everywhere, nor do other Asian people automatically represent Nate's beliefs. But even more importantly, white people who ascribe a person of color's silence in the face of blatant racist stupidity as approval of said stupidity are practicing some really solid good white racism. Just because other people don't call out your racism doesn't mean that you're not doing harm. It's very possible they are just practicing some solid survival techniques in the vast wilderness called whiteness, because when Nate challenges your racist stereotypes, he is actually putting himself in great emotional—and quite possibly, physical—danger.

"But Reverse Racism!"

Let's start here: *also not a thing*.

We've all heard the stories—a member of the BIPOC community says something insulting to white people, or a company proudly proclaims its affirmative action initiatives, and white people start feeling threatened. The next thing you know, they're claiming that they are the victims of "reverse racism," even though nothing bad has actually happened to them except maybe their feelings got hurt. I'm not discounting how bad this can feel. But relative to the effects of generations of systemic, institutionalized racism, what we might feel in these cases is miniscule to what people of color have experienced their entire lives.

To understand why reverse racism can't be a thing, we have to think systemically, not individually. It's true that people of color can have racialized thinking that causes them to develop biases, prejudices, and belief systems based on race. People of color can act like really big jerks because of those belief systems. They can also hurt other people's feelings—white people included. In fact, these people can even be abusive and possibly violent as a result of racialized thought patterns.

But that is not racism.

Many times, the things that people call reverse racism are corrections to inherently racist power structures—affirmative action is a great example of this. A conference that offers a space only for people of color—where they can go to escape the whiteness that surrounds them to refresh themselves and relax, safe from microaggressions—is often perceived as a threat or affront to white people—but it's not racism. And for the record, a Black person just doesn't want to be friends with you? Also not racism. Not even if it hurts your feelings.

Racism is about systemic power structures and the way they intersect with everyday lives. Let's say I'm out shopping for a dress, and the sales clerk is a member of the BIPOC community with highly racialized thinking. If she's been programmed by the white empire, she'll likely look at me and *not* assume that I'm there to steal something. But let's say I do, and I'm caught. Chances are that I'll receive a lighter sentence (if I'm not let off the hook with a warning) than if I were a person of color. The chances are good that as a person of color, she will not be believed as quickly or as easily as I will be. I will be given the benefit of the doubt more readily, and she will have to work harder to prove her case against me. Even if her own racialized thinking had caused her to *hate* me on sight, to make her gleefully call the police when she caught me red-handed with merchandise stuffed into my purse, the systems of power over my body and free will are almost nonexistent compared to the systems of power that regulate hers.

Meanwhile, let's say I'm allowed to go on my merry way. I'm walking down the street and pass a Black man. If I decide that I want that man to have a very bad day, I could easily call the police and file some sort of complaint about him—whether he did anything or not—and I would have an entire system of justice to back me up. From the 911 operator who facilitates my call, to the police who arrive on the scene and "just do their job," to the court system and the prison-industrial complex, there is an entire power dynamic that supports me and threatens his very life. My white whim could result in a lifetime of trouble for him. That's power, my friends. That's a sick, twisted kind of privilege that no good person should ever feel comfortable or good about having. And keep in mind: just because you never would doesn't mean you never could, or that other white people don't (see examples in the next chapter). This is the system we must work to dismantle. This is the system of institutionalized racism.

The responses discussed in this chapter are just a few of the most common justifications for racism that I've come across as I've dived deeper into this work, but the list is surely not exhaustive. My purpose for including these snapshots here is twofold: First, I want to help readers understand that situations are far more complex and nuanced than surface-level arguments often allow. Second, I hope to offer language and information for those of you who already care about doing antiracist work so that when you are confronted with these arguments, you will have a handy guide to use as you do the work of deconstruction in your conversations.

The next two chapters focus on an issue that is paramount in the antiracist movement: the way race and the justice system intersect.

Action Items

Learn: Do a deeper dive into one of the constructs discussed here so that you can discuss it in detail the next time someone uses it as a justification for racism.

Think: Which of the racist constructs detailed in this chapter have you embodied at one point or another? Can you think of others not mentioned here?

Act: The next time you hear one of these justifications being used in conversation, open your mouth and use what you've learned. Perhaps you might even practice your response ahead of time.

Chapter Seven

White People's Posse

(Or, *You Just* Think *You* Need to Call the Police)

The list is already long and is still growing: How many reasons can white people find to call the police on Black people who are just . . . being Black? Whether Black people are picnicking in a park, dozing in their dormitory common room, waiting for a friend at Starbucks, or visiting a friend's gym, a strange sort of spell seems to come over the white people in the vicinity, and for some reason, they think it's time to call the police.

Actually, who am I kidding? It's not a spell. It's *racism*—good white racism, to be exact.

But what's going on here really? Why do white people feel the need to call the police on Black people who are just living their lives, not bothering anyone, especially when white people do the same things all the time and are never perceived as a threat? I believe it has to do with two main issues: the social contract (and more specifically, the *racial* contract) and the white ownership of space.

The Racial Contract

Centuries ago, philosophers came up with the theory of the social contract—essentially, the idea that people who live in a society come to a certain unspoken agreement, in which everyone agrees to live by certain rules and to expect certain benefits and securities in return. One of the agreements we enter into as members of so-called civilization is the relinquishment of certain freedoms. As citizens, we give up the complete, individual freedom of our natural state and consent to be governed, to abide by certain laws, and to share resources. We consent because it's in our best interest; cooperation with the society at large offers us safety and security and access to resources that might be otherwise difficult to obtain, so we willingly agree not to do things like run stop signs or steal from each other. We agree to be governed and to participate in that governance, even if that's just by being upstanding citizens. Note immediately that at its essence, the social contract is about power and its relinquishment. As individuals, we give up a certain amount of power in order to enjoy the benefits of civilization.

The social contract can be divided into two subcategories: the *political* contract, in which we agree to whatever form of government our country has as well as our responsibilities as citizens, and the *moral* contract, which is the foundational code that tells us how to behave in society. Here we find basic social mores that tell us, for example, that murder and stealing are wrong. But we also find other, more fluid restrictions, such as what sexual practices are unacceptable, what clothing should not be worn in public, and when it's not cool to dance on someone else's table at a local restaurant. That last one may seem ridiculous, and it is. But it's also an example of how the unspoken social contract of morality works to control thoughts and behavior. The fact that we think the idea is ridiculous demonstrates that the moral contract defines the way we think, even if we don't notice that happening. You simply don't dance on someone else's table at a restaurant. You'd be judged as strange, and probably a jerk. And someone would probably call the cops to control your behavior and align it with the social contract. You big weirdo.

More recently, scholars have added another subcategory to the social contract—the racial contract—and here's where it gets interesting. Racial contract theory attempts to explain how certain individuals are placed in a society; it examines social hierarchy and each person's place within it. The racial contract—much like the moral contract—is both descriptive and normative. In other words, it describes how things are, but it also describes *how they should be.*[1]

There are a few important things to understand about the racial contract. First, and most obviously, it is the societal agreement that not only separates but also subordinates nonwhites from whites. This is the agreement we've all made—unconsciously, in most cases—that creates a lower civil standing for nonwhite people and that plays out in interactions BIPOC have with both the nation-state as an entity and with white people interpersonally. The purpose of the racial contract is really nothing more than self-maintenance. It's designed to benefit white people and to allow for the exploitation of BIPOC communities—their bodies (slavery), their land (think the American colonies and First Nations people), and their resources (consider the way South America has been raped for its natural resources, such as coffee, cocoa, and lumber). According to Charles W. Mills, author of *The Racial Contract*, all white people are beneficiaries of the racial contract, even if they don't necessarily agree with or desire it.

Members of the BIPOC community don't sign up for the racial contract; they don't agree to be subject to it. Rather, it is an agreement that *white people make with one another, over the non-white population.*[2] Here's where this gets really interesting: while the social contract discusses the transition of humanity from our "natural state" to the "civil/political state," the racial contract is about *our transition into whiteness or nonwhiteness.*[3] The assumption is that white people in our natural state are already "civilized," and nonwhite people are not. Nonwhite people are considered "savages," biologically somehow unable to completely assimilate into civilization—at least not without a whole lot of help. Under this construct, the "savage" nonwhites are deemed as childlike, incapable of self-rule, and wards of the state—in other words, a problem the white civilization has to manage. Remember the chapter on education, in which white teachers feel that BIPOC children require more attention in order to meet the same requirements as whites? Yeah, *that.*

Ugly Beauty + the Savage Beast: The Savage Construct

In case you're thinking that all this social contract stuff doesn't apply to you, let's do a little thought experiment. Have you ever been surprised to discover that a member of the BIPOC community, who maybe is dressed in baggy jeans and a hoodie on the day you meet them, has a PhD? Yeah, well, that feeling of surprise you have, where you're all impressed? That's the "savage construct" at work in your psyche. Ever caught yourself thinking, "Wow, she speaks really well for a Black person"? Savage construct. Ever been surprised that the immigrant from El Salvador is a lawyer? That the Black kid has two parents at home? That the Black person walking in the hallway of your fancy apartment building actually lives there? Savage. Construct.

Once whiteness uses the savage construct to infantilize the BIPOC community, we get to then feel really awesome about ourselves for dominating them for their own good. After all, it's the moral thing to do. Way back in the day, when theories of race emerged as a pseudoscience, this white European moral theory that says whiteness is naturally superior was quick to follow. (Remember Derrida and how binaries always beget hierarchies?) We saw people of color, we determined them savage and "less than," and we decided that the moral thing to do was to dominate them—for "their own good" and the good of society.

This is why racist ideologies like the savage construct are so deeply embedded in our thinking. Our white European tribal morality—remember how deep these safety mechanisms of tribal power go in our psyches—tells us that the natural state of whiteness is superior to nonwhiteness and so it is our moral responsibility to dominate anyone who is not white. Somewhere deep in our brains is this little psychic worm that tells us being *racist* is essentially *good*.

And we wonder where all these good white racists come from.

Here's another thing that, if you're like me, might make you a little sick to your stomach: This agreement we've made somewhere deep in our collective psyches that racism is actually our moral responsibility—the white empire's gift to the world—is also *a collective agreement to remain misinformed.*[4] It requires us to continue to go along with the "officially sanctioned truth" that whiteness is naturally superior rather than the objective truth, because, let's face it—and get ready to clutch your proverbial pearls—objectively there is plenty of evidence that BIPOC are perfectly normal human beings.

Shocking, I know.

It takes a consolidated effort on the part of white people to continually misinterpret the objective truth, with the understanding that our misinterpretations will be validated by white authority.[5] Think about how many unarmed Black people have been shot by police who are then found not guilty; here is our collective agreement in action. Society agrees that young Black men are dangerous and require additional force to be controlled. This misinterpretation of truth is validated with every not-guilty verdict handed down to violent, out-of-control police officers. Members of the BIPOC community who protest these misinterpretations can be ignored because of their agreed-upon lower civic standing. White people who call out these misinterpretations are understood as rebelling against their civic duty to toe the line of our collective fantasy. White people who point to the objective truth—say, that innocent people being shot by the police might indicate that *Houston, we have a problem*—are considered traitors to the tribe, to the white empire.

But what does any of this have to do with white people calling the police on BIPOC? Well, now that we understand the bug in our brains called the racial contract, we can begin to examine how that impacts the white ownership of space.

White Ownership of Space

Scholars tend to agree that the concept of race came into being at the same time the Europeans began their campaign to conquer the world. That campaign—whether we call it imperialism, colonialism, or general assholery—was, in essence, all about space. Europeans sought to go out and discover the world—a very natural human desire, and not one that is inherently evil. It's the domination part that sucks. It's the part where they said, "Once I 'discover' a land, it's mine, regardless of who might be living there." It's about the ownership of space.

The white, European thought process is a mindset of conquest and domination and taking spaces. Ownership rights rule in the minds of these conquerors, and with that ownership of land comes the right to "own" and dominate the people in those lands. Strangely enough, they did this in the name of a savior who eschewed such worldly endeavors as property ownership and domination, asked his followers to instead sell their property and give the proceeds to the poor, and said the meek would inherent the earth. (Of course, the powers that be in Jesus' day didn't much appreciate those ideas either.)

When it comes to BIPOC communities, there are a few ways that white people think about space through the lens of the racial contract theory. We might bring people of color into white spaces as so-called subordinates (think slavery and domestic servitude), we might exclude them (think reservations and ghettos), or we might deny their existence and/or exterminate them (consider the Holocaust). In general, white people tend to move freely through space but will avoid spaces they believe to be primarily Black. However, members of the BIPOC community must participate in society in order to receive its benefits like everyone else, and they must move through white spaces in order to do so.

Though white people today aren't sailing around their local communities in ships trying to conquer their neighbors' backyards, bearing grill spatulas and baffling children on their swing sets with their forced takeovers of suburban lawns, we do still like to think we own space. We may not say it outright, but every time we feel a little suspicious of a person of color, every time our brain jumps to the conclusion that a person of color must be shoplifting when they're in a fancy store or trespassing when they're in an expensive neighborhood—that's the racial construct at work within the white space. This makes driving while Black, barbecuing while Black—hell, just standing around and breathing while Black—a dangerous prospect for anyone who dares to, you know, *exist* in the skin they were born with.

Because of the savage construct that is still at work deep in our psyches, not only do we like to think we own space—especially public space—but we also like to think that it is our civic duty to police Black and Brown bodies who may be moving through white space in ways we perceive as threatening. Or even not so threatening—like, very often, not threatening at all.

As good white racists move through space, we believe that we have not just a civic duty but a *moral responsibility* to police Black and Brown bodies for their own good. Moral responsibility often trumps civic duty—look at, for example, the way religious objectors can avoid serving in the military. A moral responsibility is a deeply embedded neurobiological drive (see earlier chapters that discuss tribal think and the reticular activator) that's about survival. A moral responsibility—even one that we have collectively agreed to continuously misrepresent and believe in—is the kind of thing that can cause LGBTQIA folks to commit suicide rather than come out to their churches or parents. It can cause couples to stay in miserable marriages for decades. It can cause a whole generation of people to grow up sexually dysfunctional because of a so-called purity culture that wasn't really pure at all. In other words, these things are powerful motivators of behavior, even if they happen to be incredibly misinformed.

Now take the white empire's approved set of behaviors and coded language, and bring them into the public space. When BIPOC move through those same public spaces and perform behaviors that in any way seem out of the norm of prescribed whiteness, the good white racist will respond with an attempt to regain the status quo. We have an entire justice system ready to back us up, and we're not afraid to use it.

In fact, we have been programmed to use it. Police shows on television and gang member in movies suggest the inherent criminality of Black and Brown bodies. The newscasts that show mug shots of Black perpetrators and yearbook photos of white perpetrators reinforces this imagery. Our good white racist tendencies—the ones that make us think it's our moral responsibility to maintain law and order over the BIPOC community for their own good—make us think that it's perfectly acceptable and normal to call police when Black and Brown bodies are simply moving through white spaces.

Like most discussions about race, this is all about white comfort levels, and sameness breeds comfort. When a white person walks into a Starbucks and sits down to wait for a business prospect to arrive before ordering, most white managers barely even notice, much less call the police. I mean, the idea seems ridiculous. I can't tell you how many business meetings I've had in coffee shops where I never bought anything until my guest arrived. But two Black men—what with their inherent criminality, their lower civic status, the obvious savage traits they are exhibiting by sitting there minding their own business in their button-up shirts and their khakis—obviously, these men are a threat. The police must be called.

Here is where the agreed-upon misinformation of the racial contract comes into play in the white collective psyche—a group fantasy in which, despite all evidence to the contrary, whiteness is superior to nonwhiteness. And when the police arrive on the scene and remove the two Black men instead of fining the white manager for wasting the officers' time, that's whiteness affirming the collective fantasy. That's the societal agreement to remain misinformed at work.

That's some solid good white racism right there.

What's important to notice here is the system at play. Everyone is participating in the fantastical white world of misinformation, from store managers who are not only more suspicious of Black and Brown bodies but who also have higher expectations of them than they do of white people, to the police who automatically assume the white manager is in the right. In this real-life example, in which two Black men were arrested for sitting in a Starbucks without buying anything while they waited for a friend, they were also denied access to the bathroom because they had not made a purchase. Meanwhile, a white woman claimed she had been at the Starbucks for hours and not bought anything.[6]

The manager—a white person in a position of authority through having dominion over this space—called the police, who did not question the manager's story but simply told the two men they had to leave. The police did not seek the men's side of the story or ask them questions. They ignored the other customers in the store—many of whom were white—who told them the men had done nothing wrong. The officers simply sided with the store manager, affirmed the misinformation she was perpetuating, and arrested the men. Here, whiteness used the justice system to back up the racial contract, affirm the "official truth of misinformation," and maintain the white person's comfort level. This is a congruence of power systems, both tangible and intangible, that impact the freedoms of Black and Brown bodies while privileging those assigned whiteness, because white people never have the police called on them for just sitting in a Starbucks.

When it comes to power and its abuses, these kinds of stories are myriad and frustrating for their obvious racist tendencies. But for the BIPOC community, they could become nothing short of deadly. For most of us, the police are the first—and for white people, often the only—experience with the criminal justice system. Most middle-class white people tend to have a healthy respect for police, to see them as characters in a Norman Rockwell painting, in which the friendly beat officer tips his hat and buys the lost kid an ice cream cone. The BIPOC community does not have the same experience.

My friend Stefan is a Black man with a career as a public defender as long as his dreadlocks. He is a family man who not only attends church regularly but also mentors youth, paints in his spare time, and leads a busy, suburban life. One hot summer day, while driving home from vacation wearing the seasonal wardrobe of shorts and a T-shirt, his family in the car with him, he got pulled over. He told me, "Kerry, the only thing I could think of was *Is this the day my little girl sees me get murdered by the police?*" He knew through the entire incident that keeping his hands on the wheel was an issue of life or death. When it was over, he felt a rush of relief and, at the same time, the fear of what might have been.

White people do not have this type of fear in dealings with the police.

Not only do we not have this kind of fear—we can't even begin to understand it. But we do know it exists in the minds and hearts of the BIPOC community, and that's what we're counting on every time we call the police on a person living while Black. Though we may not be aware of what we're doing at the time (except for, you know, those times when we're totally aware of it), there is a not-so-subtle power dynamic that we are taking advantage of when we police the bodies of people of color in public space. It's sticking the flag in the space and saying we own it. It's reminding them who actually has the power.

That's why the slate of "while Black" stories in which white people call the police on Black people just living their lives is about so much more than mistaken identity or a lapse of judgment. It's nothing short of racial terrorism. It is the modern day, good white racist's form of cross burning. Except our crosses wear blue. They carry guns and billy clubs, badges and handcuffs.

Our crosses, like the original instrument of Jesus' execution, are agents of the state.

Action Items

Learn: Learn about the many "while Black" stories to get a true understanding of the magnitude of the problem.

Think: How would you feel if you were policed the way the BIPOC community is policed in public spaces? Does it feel strange or dangerous to you to think about it? Do you have different standards for people of color than you do for white people in public spaces?

Act: Prepare an action plan for if you ever find yourself in a place where a person of color is being policed "while Black." How will you show up as an ally? Thinking about this ahead of time will make it more likely that you will act in the moment.

Chapter Eight

Unequal Justice

(Or, *Liberty and Justice for All White People and White People Only*)

Recently I passed a billboard that had a picture of a friendly looking police officer and the following admonishment to parents: "Stop Telling Your Children to Fear Us. We Want Them to Run TO Us, Not From Us." While I understand this sentiment, it made me a little angry. I was not the target audience for this billboard, of course. I teach my children that the police are their friends, and for my children—my *white* children—it's true. As middle class, suburban kids growing up white in America, my kids are privileged this way. I am privileged to be able to tell my kids to go to the police when they need help.

But that does not tell the whole story about the justice system in America. Not even close.

Most Black moms don't have the luxury of painting a quaint picture of the quintessential American cop for their kids. What most Black moms have to do is get real. They have to teach their children how to survive an interaction with the police. I have the inherent, privileged ability to move myself right out of that little nightmare into the Norman Rockwell daydream of whiteness.

Please don't tell me I'm anticop, because this situation is nuanced and complex and at other times blatant and outrageous; one thing it is definitely not is simple. There are a lot of reasons why innocent Black people being shot by the police is a very bad thing for cops, and it's not just about troublesome PR. But the police are just one cog in the broken wheel of justice that continuously oppresses the BIPOC community.

Maybe that's why I felt a certain way about that billboard. It's smiling face—carefully selected, I'm guessing, for its racial ambiguity—did not just represent a refusal to acknowledge the chasm of justice that exists between Black people and the police force, but it also *blamed Black people for the problem.* It said, "It's your fault that Black people are afraid of us, because you keep telling Black kids to be fearful" rather than acknowledging the role police have—and have had, historically—in the rift between the BIPOC community and the justice system. It's not just the police, of course. The system begins with the police, but it includes the courts and the prison system too. And race rears its ugly head at every turn.

This is the system of white empire that operates just under the radar of good white racists—and most of us like it that way. It's a world most of us don't really need to be concerned with, but it's also a world that feeds on human lives, where the good American ideal of liberty and justice for all doesn't seem to exist, and Black and Brown bodies bear the brunt of its brute force. What's even more disturbing is that there is an entire economy built around the constructed criminality of the BIPOC community, and it serves the financial interests of the white empire. So if we're good people, how can this be happening right under our noses? Whole books have been written about the topic, and honestly, it takes an entire book—or two—to unpack it. My goal here is to help you #NoticeTheSystem and how our whiteness—yours and mine—helps us participate in its injustice, because I know that as good people, once we see evil things, we'll want to do something about them.

We've already established that when white people claim they don't see race, they're really attempting to avoid a racialized experience. But there's something a little more insidious happening here, because when you get a bunch of white people together who claim they don't see race, that means they can also claim they don't see *racism.* When we decide that race isn't a *thing,* that has societal implications. We can then justify—to our family at the dinner table and to the collective with our votes—higher arrest and conviction rates for people of color and think to ourselves, "Don't do the crime if you can't do the time." We can tell ourselves it's not because of race, because race isn't a thing. Color blindness allows racism to occur and then points in the other direction.[1] It allows us collectively to stay misinformed and comfortable. The justice system is arguably the most racist institution in America, so of course it's easier not to examine. But since we're good, we're going to take a look at its three components: the police, the courts, and the prison system.

The Police

There is no doubt that when cops are killed in the line of duty, it is a horrible thing. Police officers endure huge amounts of stress, and their families carry a burden of worry and fear that seems unfair. Brave men and women put themselves on the line and in danger every day as part of the social contract to which we've all agreed. This is no small thing, and as Nadine Smith, a reporter turned social activist, pointed out when we spoke on the *White on White* podcast, a cop killer deserves a harsher punishment because of the social contract. Not only has a cop killer violated the moral code to do no harm, but this person has attacked the basic fabric of our society and its safety.

Nadine also points out that the social contract must go both ways. Police officers who break protocols or practice a form of state-authorized vigilantism need to be held to a higher standard too, as agents of the state. This is imperative for maintaining social confidence in our collective agreement. When that confidence fades, the social fabric of our society gets ripped to shreds. In America, a sacred trust has been broken between our government and a portion of our community, and people are dying because of it. But rather than honestly look at that reality, good white racists jump up and down yelling things like "Don't talk about it during the football game!" or "But Black-on-Black crime!"

My friend Lisa, who in addition to being a former police officer is also a veteran of the armed services, explained something I believe needs to be a matter of urgent national concern. She said, "There is a lot of talk about veterans coming home from war with PTSD, and that's good that we're talking about it. But every day, police officers see absolutely horrific things, and as soon as that call is done, they're off to the next one. No one is caring for these officers. No one is treating them for PTSD. They are just being sent out over and over again to deal with the next horrible thing." Which makes giving them a gun probably not so much a good idea.

The way Lisa describes it, the police force is also like a big, dysfunctional family, intent on keeping the family secret. As in any workplace, there are what she calls bad apples—officers who simply shouldn't be on the job and have the record to prove it. They are few and far between, but they are also the ones that generate headlines *because they actually kill people.* There is no system in place to ensure that these cops don't get back into uniform, even after they've killed unarmed citizens. "Show me almost any bad shooting," she says, "and I can show you a file on that cop that would tell you this was coming from a mile away." There is a blue wall of silence that keeps good cops from calling out the bad ones, and that keeps these officers on the job, armed, and dangerous.

I believe part of this comes from the pressure to maintain the American good guy–bad guy duality, this idea that America is good, that we win every war, and that every agent of our state is a noble hero. But then how do we explain that Black people are three times as likely to be killed by police than white people, and that in 2015, for example, white victims were 10 percent more likely to be armed than Black victims?[2]

What do good white people do with this information?

I say that we need to care for our cops. We need to care enough about our cops that we should worry that some of them are being transformed into murderers. I say we should be concerned about the fact that their souls are being destroyed by what they experience, and we should tender care and treatment to them.

I say that as good people, we should be infuriated that our justice system is, apparently, totally okay with the fact that certain people, based on the color of their skin, are killed three times as often by agents of the state as white people are. I think we should care about this. I honestly don't know how good people can ignore this.

And if you are a cop? I think you should be *infuriated*. Because so many of you are good. So many of you have the right intentions. But you've been played by a system that wants to use you to perpetrate injustice. It may not be your fault. But it's absolutely your responsibility.

I wonder where our sense of collective rage has gone, as a society whose fabric is shredding before our eyes, whose citizens are dying on the daily. Is there not a single person of color in your life that you love, that prompts you to think, *Holy shit, this could be them?* Is there not one person you care about who falls into this category, whom you love deeply enough that a part of you would break a little if they were shot down in the street for something as simple, as normal, as maybe selling a cigarette? Walking to 7-11 to buy some Skittles? Forgetting to signal a turn? Having a broken taillight, and then telling the officer they are licensed to carry a gun, and when they follow directions and reach for their identification, they are murdered in cold, panicked blood?

The Courts

Mike was a kid with big, shiny cheeks and a bigger smile. He was one of my favorites—usually friendly and easy-going, though sometimes he let his emotions get the best of him and he'd act out. He was one of the kids in the mentoring program I had the pleasure of running for about a year and a half when I was on staff at my local church as the community involvement director. The kids in the program were at-risk youth on probation. That's the polite way to say it. The reality is that most of the kids were gang members—except they weren't hardened, tough gang members. Really, they were just kids.

Statistics show that Black people—including kids like Mike—are incarcerated at a rate 5.1 times higher than the rate for white people.[3] Researchers have identified three main reasons for this:

policies and practices that drive disparity, implicit bias, and structural disadvantages among communities of color.

Policies related to the War on Drugs have overwhelmingly impacted communities of color. Blacks are four times as likely to be arrested for drug offenses as whites—though both groups use drugs at roughly the same rate—and are more likely to be detained under stop-and-frisk policies, often for nothing more than "furtive behavior."[4] This often leads to unnecessary criminal records for thousands, which in turn leads to harsher punishments for their "habitual offender" status. Implicit bias comes into play in arrest policies as well as sentencing, where the savage construct creates perceptions of Black and Brown bodies as more threatening, which results in harsher sentences. Sound familiar? Here is the white empire at work, ready to control Black and Brown bodies "for their own good." Meanwhile, structural and social factors, such as poverty, unemployment or underemployment, housing disparities, and family differences all contribute to a higher incarceration rate for Blacks.[5] Segregated communities in inner-city neighborhoods that experience a high degree of violent crime increase the likelihood of an encounter with the criminal justice system and, therefore, incarceration.

In other words, for no reason other than the place, class, and color of skin they were born into, kids like Mike get funneled through a system that practically spits them out in front of the court's door. Once they're there, they become victims of one of America's biggest sins we never talk about: the prison-industrial complex.

The Prison System

Before we start to unpack the American prison system, we must first acknowledge a very important fact: constitutionally speaking, *slavery is still legal in America*. While the Thirteenth Amendment abolished the institution of slavery, it allowed for one important exception: slave labor can still be forced upon convicted criminals as punishment for their crimes.

You've probably heard the terms "mass incarceration" and "the prison-industrial complex" bantered about by talking heads on your news channel. I never gave much thought to what these terms actually meant; they sounded like highly technical legal terms that had nothing to do with me. In fact, they are components of a legalized system of slavery that very likely produces actual products you and I use every day. Go ahead and ask Google to tell you what companies use prison labor in their supply chain. You might be surprised.

In her groundbreaking book *The New Jim Crow*, Michelle Alexander expertly lays out the myriad ways the American justice system is essentially creating a new caste system, with Black convicts at the bottom and corporate profiteers at the top. Criminality has become big business, with monetary incentives to increase the number of incarcerated people in order to fill the pockets of investors in for-profit prisons. Call me crazy, but I can't for the life of me think that having a financial incentive to lock up more people could possibly be good idea.

But in a twisted and corrupt capitalist society, that's exactly what's happening. According to Alexander, a 2005 annual report for the Corrections Corporation of America plainly states that the company needs to build and fill more prisons to survive and would be adversely affected by more lenient sentencing policies, the relaxation of enforcement, or the decriminalization of certain activities.[6] So if you're wondering why your state hasn't yet legalized that joint you've got stuffed in a shoebox in your closet, you might want to see if you can figure out what corporations are lobbying your state legislature. Chances are, they have a vested interest in keeping marijuana illegal because the arrests and convictions fill their coffers with revenue generated by prisoners' labor, most of whom are Black and Brown.

Once in prison, those bodies can be legally sold to the highest bidder for cheap labor. A prisoner sold through a convict-leasing program may have sewn your underwear, picked your vegetables, or shrink-wrapped your computer mouse. Most likely, at least a few of the consumer products you and I enjoy have probably been touched by modern-day slave labor. And good people like you and me justify it by thinking to ourselves, "Oh, well. They're criminals, after all." Except they're not all criminals—judges have been caught literally selling kids to the prison system for offenses like mocking a principal or cursing at a friend's mom. In Pennsylvania, for example, judges accepted bribes from the for-profit companies that run the state's prisons in exchange for funneling kids into their facilities for minor offenses.[7]

That's the kind of evil a for-profit prison system perpetrates.

A conviction is not just a social stigma; it's a green light for legal discrimination and can impact housing, employment, and the right to vote, to give just a few examples.[8] These obstacles make reentry into productive citizenship difficult at best, and they predominantly affect the BIPOC community.

I am guilty of being apathetic about this subject for the sheer massiveness of the problem. It feels hopeless, except there is one thing in my favor: you. And me.

With the power we have as white people—if we combined our money and our votes and our collective voices—we could actually change this system. We could do better. We could practice a radical act of reparation, and in the process, maybe—just maybe—we could redeem our own white souls.

Action Items

Learn: Is there a for-profit prison in your state? Is there a prison reform bill on the table? What does it say? Become an informed citizen. While you're at it, be sure to Google the list of companies that are using prison labor.

Think: Who benefits from mass incarceration, the prison-industrial complex, and the convict-leasing program?

Act: Write to the companies you discover use prison labor, and express your desire for them to invest the savings they receive from that into postprison reentry programs for the prisoners released from the facilities with which they have contracts.

Chapter Nine

The Consumption of Bodies

(Or, *"Step Away from the Hair"*)

White America has a consumption problem. From our earliest European beginnings, we have been a wide-open mouth, an insatiable gullet that believes the world is our oyster, to slurp down in one big, selfish gulp. This manifests in any number of ways sociologically, economically, internationally, ecologically, politically, interpersonally. Like everything else I've been talking about so far, the empire reaches far and wide, from the macro environment of global politics to the conversation you're having with your family and friends over wine or coffee. As the dominant culture, we consume Black and Brown bodies as quickly and easily as we consume the trees from which our paper is pressed, the coffee grown on trees that aren't ours, the cotton we've never spent a day picking in our lives. Black and Brown women, children, and people who belong to the LGBTQIA community are at particular risk, though no Black and Brown people walk this earth with the privilege of assumed safety, and Black men move through American space with a particular kind of threat at their backs.

Because Everything Is Ours

The area known as Hayti in Durham, North Carolina, was a thriving neighborhood filled with a well-educated Black middle class, Black-owned businesses, and a tight-knit sense of community.

Surrounded by white communities—with white churches—the neighborhood housed a Black Wall Street and the Mutual Life Company, one of the largest Black-owned businesses and a potent symbol of Black wealth. But during the 1960s, as the automobile began to change the way Americans lived and traveled, the government decided it needed a freeway. In order to preserve the white churches that existed all over Durham County, the government planned for the freeway to cut directly through idyllic Hayti, which decimated businesses and required leveling homes and relocating churches and other important centers of community. This story has been played out repeatedly all over the country—white need and greed decimating Black spaces, consuming them for our own needs, and forcing Black and Brown bodies to move and rearrange themselves according to our whims. The land bears the same scars as the people, with gaping voids where wealth and abundance once flowed, like the leftover pickings of a great banquet after all the guests have gone. Only this actor was no welcomed guest; it was the pillaging gullet of the beast of whiteness and its systemic power, and the scraps it left were barely fit for the rats that lived in the untended yards of the community it decimated.

This past Black History Month, when I opened my email inbox for a quick perusal of what usually amounts to nothing more than a giant pile of spam, I was greeted with a plethora of emails from retailers exclaiming, "It's Black History Month!" and offering me deals on all sorts of Black-authored books, Black-made products, and paraphernalia celebrating Black activists. While I celebrate the promotion of products created by Black people, I cringe at the commodification of Black History Month, because I'm pretty sure that the bulk of the dollars are landing in corporate pockets with pale-skinned investors. Black History Month, intended to honor and recognize the history and achievements of African Americans, has now also become a marketing ploy to invite more dollars into the hands of retail businesses that are not, generally, owned or run by people of color. The commodification of Black History Month speaks to the way we as a culture love to consume Blackness but don't necessarily want to create equal space for

Blackness to exist as its own entity, as valuable as anything that might be white. Until there are Black and Brown voices regularly being highlighted as prominently as white voices in every promotional email that goes out, we still have a long way to go. If Black History Month is going to be used to sell products, the profits should fill the pockets—both proverbial and literal—of Black people, not the already abundant coffers of wealthy white investors. In other words, not much has changed since the so-called Age of Discovery (see chapter 2). We still think everything is ours by divine right.

The Doctrine of Dominion

The Christian doctrine of dominion is based in the book of Genesis (Gen. 1:26, to be exact) and states that God gave dominion over the earth to humankind. Combined with some nasty supersessionist theology that reallocates Old Testament promises to Christ and Christians, church leaders began teaching that not *all* of humanity was granted dominion—just Christians.[1] I don't know about you, but I find a certain hubris in the idea that only Christians have been granted dominion over all creation—and I'm a Christian. I have a problem with this thinking because when we say that Christians are the only humans with dominion over all of creation, then *other humans fall subject to that dominion.*

This thinking got into bed with the political and economic interests of Europeans during the so-called Age of Discovery and created lovely little institutions like slavery. The concept of white dominion over Black and Brown bodies is deeply embedded in the Christian faith, and it's deeply embedded in the psychological constructs of whiteness. Ultimately, the concept of dominion leads to exploitation, most clearly demonstrated by the institution of slavery, obviously. *But slavery is over*, people say. *Jim Crow is abolished, and segregation is a thing of the past.*

Not so fast there, Skippy.

If you haven't yet noticed it, let me point it out for you. There is still a sense among white people that whiteness is in charge, that the BIPOC cultures and the styles and the ways of being in the world are ours for the taking. In addition to the obvious form this has taken—slavery, the theft of land—it has taken other forms as well. The minstrel show, for example, exploited the stereotypes of Black bodies for the entertainment of rich, landowning men, and imagery born from the minstrel show and from colonialism in general is still used today to sell rice (Uncle Ben's), pancake mix and syrup (Aunt Jemima and Mrs. Butterworth), and bananas (Chiquita). Here is where the idea of Black and Brown bodies being consumed by whiteness becomes almost literal. When we consider the narrative arc of enslaved Africans, stolen from their homeland to work in American fields to help produce our food and clothing, we begin to associate them with our own nourishment. As slaves moved into more domestic spheres, working in kitchens to prepare our meals and even taking care of and nursing white children, the idea of consumption and nourishment dug an even deeper trench into our collective unconscious. It is not hard to understand, then, why my mother has such a love for the "mammy" imagery from her childhood, even though she never had a Black caretaker herself. It represents a maternalism and sense of nurturing that to her doesn't feel evil or wrong. It simply feels like love to a child who had no idea that her nurturing was coerced and stolen. My mother had no idea she was receiving a phony, contraband love in the form of racist marketing practices. She simply received with eagerness the pancakes and syrup or buttered rice, associated them with stereotyped Blackness, and felt satisfied, cared for, and happy. Her good white racism was successfully embedded into her brain with every bite, and it felt good while it went down.

When we put the face of a First Nations person on a T-shirt, complete with sacred ritual headdress, and refer to that image as a mascot, that is the consumption of Black and Brown bodies and culture by whiteness. That is the remnant of the colonial mindset that says, "We came, we took the land, we own everything in it, and we can therefore take your culture and use it however we want." From the "Just shut up and entertain me" response to the Take a Knee movement to the "Shut up and dribble" mentality toward NBA players, this is American white consumerism at its worst. We're fine with Black people entertaining us, but God forbid they have an opinion.

You're Cool Because of Your Black Friend

We practice the consumption of Black and Brown bodies when we claim that our BIPOC friend absolves us of racism. Every time we claim our own coolness by proxy, we are centering our own whiteness and saying that everything else—including our friend's Blackness—serves it and serves us. We are using their identity to affirm our white goodness. Sometimes we even think that our relationality with people of color allows us to touch them in, frankly, weird ways, such as touching their hair. For the record, that's just creepy.

Strangely, while we've fetishized BIPOC bodies, we also have policed them, subjecting them to a beauty standard based on how our own bodies look and move in space. BIPOC culture—whether it's African American, First Nations, Korean, or Latinx culture—has become something exotic and othered (note how whiteness is still centered here) and something to be both controlled and utilized at our pleasure, maybe for an "edgy" hairstyle or party theme. This is not just about white people stealing and appropriating other cultures—it's about actual, real harm being done to the BIPOC community by our actions.

Meanwhile, when young girls are kicked out of school because of the way their hair grows out of their heads or because their hairstyle is considered "distracting" (while white women appropriate the style for themselves and are lauded for being fashion-forward) that, my friends, is privilege screaming in your ear, saying, *I'm white, and I'm more powerful than you.* And good people don't normally go around wielding power over other people. (Or do we?)

From our ridiculous celebrations of Cinco de Mayo and St. Patrick's Day as excuses to drink to excess and attempt dialects or accents we should leave to indigenous speakers, to the way we appropriate traditional Chinese dresses and use them for our prom fashion, white Americans have a sense of entitlement, a belief that what personal freedom actually means is the right to take whatever we happen to come across as we go gallivanting through the world, including other people's bodies, languages, and cultures. When immigrants come to our shores, we are happy to use their bodies to pluck our vegetables from fields but are not so happy to give them a living wage to buy food for their own families. We've spent a lot of time building and maintaining the savage construct to describe the people who surround us, when all along it actually seems the savage beast is us. We work hard and well at a savage sort of goodness that leaves nothing but destruction in its wake. And we smile nicely while we do it.

Most good white racists have no idea that we participate in this type of savagery. After all, we like to think of ourselves as good. We move through the world assuming the BIPOC community loves us as much as we love to appropriate their culture. White people like me often think of our friendship as a gift we can throw around like candy from a parade float, generously and indiscriminately, and that everyone on the sidelines will clamor for it. This isn't necessarily true. The thing we must learn—what I learned, the hard way—is that our friendship is not a gift to be given out. Friendship is something to be earned. But allyship?

That's our responsibility, as is the requirement that we learn to do it right.

On Friends and Comrades

Paula was one of the friendliest people I've ever met. She smiled with her whole face—eyes sparkling, light Brown skin shining, and a deep, throaty laugh that instantly made you feel as if she thought you were the coolest person in the room. As someone who has been told over and over again that I am intimidating and unapproachable (which makes people who actually know me laugh hysterically), I admired Paula for her easy warmth and open friendliness. We would often speak of our respective heritages— she often traveled back to Uruguay, which she half-jokingly called "the land of her people," and I would share stories of my Irish ancestors and their journey to the Americas.

One of the things I noticed about Paula is that when she met someone she would say, "Hello, friend." This simple phrase seemed to instantly dissolve boundaries, setting up a foundation of ease and openness that allowed relationality to manifest organically, like a flower growing up out of the seam of a concrete sidewalk. It was beautiful, the way she did that, and I wanted to emulate it. As I began to do the self-work of becoming more vulnerable in the world, of letting go of the armor that made me intimidating and unapproachable, I chose to learn from Paula. I started to call people friend. After all, the desire to be a friend to the world can't be such a bad thing, right?

Well, maybe. And maybe not.

Dr. Robyn Henderson-Espinoza is a queer activist, Latinx scholar, and public theologian I interviewed remotely for the *White on White* podcast. I loved our conversation; it was rich and meaningful, and it felt to me as if we'd really connected. We spoke on that episode about how people as different as the two of us are can find communion over something as simple as a shared meal, and we talked about how we would love to do that in real life together someday. We tried a few times over the course of the next few months, but it never happened.

A few weeks later, I was having an abysmal day. I was at my parents' house. I was preparing for a week of travel and had a lot of work to do before I left. Of course, I also had to make sure everyone had fun on the annual trip to Grandma's. To make matters worse, on this particular hot and un-air-conditioned Wednesday, I woke up to a cracked computer screen.

Then I walked into the kitchen.

My mom was in the early stages of dementia, and she and my dad were suffering all the symptoms of aging, including not being able to see or smell as well as they used to. When I got into the kitchen, my daughter was standing next to a cabinet with a grimace on her face. "What's that smell?" she said. I moved closer to her and sniffed the aroma of rotting food. Let me point out that this was all happening *before* coffee. There's something extra special about having to clean up a rotten, liquified bag of potatoes first thing in the morning—before coffee.

After that mess was taken care of, I made a note to myself to hire a cleaning service for my parents, got my coffee, and headed back to the bedroom to try to find a way to work on a broken laptop. On my way, I opened up Twitter.

The night before, Dr. Robyn, whose preferred pronouns are they/them/their,[2] had tweeted something about an event they were headed to having to do with theology and beer; my friend Anne tagged me in her reply, saying she wished she could be there but that she would be with me in Indiana for school. I replied, saying, "One of these days, my friend, a meal together. One of these days . . ."

Now, still squirming from the potato debacle, still waiting for the caffeine to enter my bloodstream, I saw that Dr. Robyn had replied. "Well, to be clear, we don't even know one another, so isn't 'friend' a bit presumptuous?"

Ouch.

My whiteness and I were very taken aback, though that's not how I thought of it at the time. Back then, I was simply hurt. Didn't Dr. Robyn understand that by calling them a friend, I had nothing but good intentions? Didn't they know I'm a good person who wants to be an ally? DIDN'T THEY KNOW WHAT KIND OF DAY I WAS HAVING?

But here's the thing: although my feelings are valid, the perspective feeding them is not. Also, they are not the point.

I immediately apologized. I deserve no kudos for this; it was simply self-preservation in the face of what felt like a very public shaming. I wanted to avoid looking more dumb than I already did. I said, "I am truly sorry if I offended. I consider people friends until I have reason to consider otherwise. You are correct—we have not met in person. I do hope you'll always consider me a friendly face, however. Best to you." *Please God, let this conversation be over now.* Every extra character was an opportunity for me to make another mistake, and I was not even sure I understood the one I'd already made.

Trust me when I say I wanted to defend myself. I wanted to shout all over the interwebz that Dr. Robyn and I had had a wonderful conversation on the podcast and that we'd been trying to make dinner plans, so my desire for friendship and a shared meal wasn't actually as presumptuous as it may have seemed. I wanted to demonstrate my goodness and my friendly intentions to Twitterland, to all the people who were tagged in that conversation. I wanted people to understand that I was having a horrible day, and that I didn't deserve that, and that Robyn's words were hurtful.

But again, none of that is the point.

Dr. Robyn continued: "It's just that white folks have a habit of assuming particular relationality when there has been no defining of relationality. As a Latinx, I take friendship seriously, but it's not friendship I'm after with people. I need comrades, because I'm trying to help us all get free!"

In that moment, I appreciated the explanation, but I was still stung. Do they think that just because I'm white, I don't take friendship seriously? I took issue with that, especially because I care deeply and want to work out my allyship in healthy ways that actually benefit the people I want to come alongside (as opposed to propping up my own ego and doing further harm). I am serious about friendship and intentionally offer it out of a desire to self-identify as a safe place for marginalized people. When I meet someone from an oppressed community, I know that my social location as a white, cis-gendered, straight, middle-class woman makes me unsafe for them in a multitude of ways. I know that I have to do the work of earning trust and relationship, and that my whiteness is a barrier to that effort that I must acknowledge. I also know that despite my best intentions, I can still do harm even if I don't want to when I participate in a system I don't see or understand and then that system inserts itself into the relationship I'm currently embodying. Marginalized communities know this about me—about us (you, me, white people)—and they take the necessary precautions. As members of the dominant culture, it's our job to be patient, to do the work, to learn the lessons, to earn relationship and understand that no matter how hard we try, we might not ever actually be the safest place for the people with whom we are in solidarity.

Calling people friend was my way of trying to be intentional about taking that first step of relationality with people who don't share my privilege. It was my olive branch, my way of self-identifying as a white person who wants to do better, who is at least slightly aware of her own privilege and wants to use it to smash the systems of hierarchy, supremacy, and oppression that have harmed communities all over the world. Encapsulated in that one little word is all the passion I have about righting these wrongs, about correcting injustice, about healing the world of all the isms. And hell, if I'm going to be real (and if I'm not going to be real, what's the point?) it's as much a plea for inclusion as it is a battle cry. It's a request to be liked, to be seen, to be cared for as much as it is anything, because I've never felt like I fit in anywhere, with anyone, and when I find a soul who might get that, I confess I desire relationship, even when I pretend I don't. I'm annoying and complicated that way.

But one last time, for the people in the back: *None of this is the point.*

My intentions don't matter if they participate in and perpetuate the consumption of Black and Brown bodies, even metaphorically. I realize now that my presumption of friendship did not offer Dr. Robyn the opportunity to say yes to a relationship with me; it just assumed they'd want one. My feelings of hurt and indignation come from my own assumption that *of course* they'd want a relationship with me—why the hell not? I mean, aren't I #WhiteAndAwesome?

Here is an opportunity to again #NoticeTheSystem, because privilege is definitely at play here. Interestingly, when I told this story to some of my white friends, they had similar reactions across a wide range of forcefulness. Some of them vehemently protested Dr. Robyn's treatment of me. Most of them were taken aback and affirmed that they too would have been stung by their words. Almost all of them said they would have made the same mistake, which makes me realize that there is indeed a system at play here, a dynamic reality of whiteness that white people don't notice but that everyone else does.

It may help to clarify if we shift the scenario a bit. Many women I know, including myself, have experienced unwanted advances from a man, and when those advances are rejected, somehow we are made to feel bad, or guilty, or as if we are somehow wrong. In actuality, we're just not interested. Women have been socialized to pick our battles when it comes to unwanted flirtation and advances—even unwanted hands on our asses—because we don't want to "make a scene" or "be the bitch" or "hurt his feelings." After all, he's just being "nice," and I should "appreciate the compliment." This comes from a system of social dominance that privileges male (especially white male) comfort and satisfaction over and above that of any other group. If a woman doesn't appreciate a man's interest in her, something must obviously be wrong with *her*.

In the situation with Dr. Robyn, I'm like every fragile man who didn't know how to take no for an answer, who vilified the object of my desire for having the nerve to be uninterested. This, of course, was not my intention. Just like men have been socialized to believe they are entitled to have dominion over everything in their realm, I've been socialized to believe that being nice to people in marginalized communities is enough to make them want relationship with me. But the history of consumption of marginalized people by my dominant culture makes my presumption of relationship—no matter how well intended—harmful.

A guy who really respects women—including the woman he's interested in but who has rejected him—will be able to sit in the paradox of the personal pain of that rejection and the objective belief that he is not owed relationship from anyone. The man who truly honors all people will recognize that one woman's lack of romantic interest in him does not make all women entitled, cold-hearted man-eaters. It's like a person who is not thirsty when you present them with a glass of water; they're simply declining an offer.

I get to feel the sting of Dr. Robyn's rejection of my friendship—after all, feelings are valid even if their perception is skewed. What I don't get to do is linger there and decide that I will no longer do the work of true allyship because my precious feelings got hurt. I don't get to ignore the system of privilege that was at play, and I don't get to throw a temper tantrum (even though I wanted to, even though one felt—inaccurately—justified).

What I *do* get to do is imagine a way in which my intentions can lead to behavior that is not experienced as harmful by the very people I seek to stand alongside. Of course, there's another assumption I'm making there—that my intentions are truly about doing actual good and creating positive change in the world and not just about feeling better about myself. If all I care about is how I'm perceived, how I feel, and whether I'm "good," I'm not doing the work of true white allyship, nor am I being a good white person. If I truly care about dismantling privilege, I'll learn the lesson Dr. Robyn is offering, hurt feelings be damned. And the first step in doing that is to listen to the person I have harmed, lay down my defensiveness, and *learn* how they would prefer to be in relationship with me—even if that's not at all.

If Dr. Robyn wants comrades, then a comrade I will be.

Action Steps

Learn: Research some of the historically Black neighborhoods in your area. Can you identify times in their history that they were consumed by whiteness?

Think: Have you ever used products, enjoyed entertainments, or embraced fashion choices that appropriate the cultures of BIPOC communities? Have you ever used a relationship with a member of the BIPOC community to justify yourself or to absolve yourself of racism?

Act: When interacting with a person of color, don't assume relationality. This could mean assuming that someone feels safe with you before knowing you, wants relationship with you just because that's what you want, or knows you're an ally before you've acted like one. Wait to be invited into relationship, and understand that trust needs to be earned.

Chapter Ten

Shiny Happy People

(Or, *When Good White Racists Go to Church*)

ere is how the story was told to me: Deep in the bowels of a large Methodist church in the South, there are stacks of detailed minutes—reports on all the committee meetings for all the years of the life of this church about all the things. Buried in those stacks, in the papers from the era of the civil rights movement, is a dark moment in the history of this church that now stands as a beacon for social justice in its community. Though the church's steps are now draped in rainbow flags and its ministers are active social organizers for racial and economic justice, those steps were once the place of a highly symbolic and deeply disturbing incident that perfectly demonstrates the paradoxical nature of this church—and church in general.[1]

Back in those days, churches were officially segregated (unlike these days, when they are unofficially segregated). There was a small group of civil rights workers—both Black and white—who would walk to this large, imposing, and very white church every Sunday and then kneel in the back during worship and pray in a peaceful protest of the segregation of the body of Christ.

And all the white folk freaked out.

There was much clutching of pearls and many hyperventilating church ladies. *What are they doing? Why are they praying? Their kneeling is so disruptive!* Hours of committee meetings were spent discussing what to do. How to handle this diverse group of people

131

who had the gall to want to kneel in church and pray together? Then on one Communion Sunday, the members of the group decided that they were not going to remain in the back of the church, but walk down the aisle and take Communion together at the table of Christ. You know—kind of like Jesus meant it to be.

The white people were extra freaked out. This could *not* be allowed to happen. Not *Communion*! Knowing that if the civil rights workers made it into the church that day they'd actually want to take Communion too, the church made a decision. As the small group of people approached the huge doors of the church, they were met not with the radical, open-door hospitality of Jesus. Instead, when the people inside saw them coming, they slammed the entrance to the church shut and locked the doors.

But outside on the steps, someone had a key to the church's back door. They snuck in, stole some bread and wine, and outside the locked doors, right there on the outermost edges of the so-called sacred space, Black and white people held Communion together with their beautifully stolen elements. The radical hospitality of Jesus is always found on the edges, outside the precious places, in the real sacred spaces where you find the people who have been shut out, marginalized, othered.

For about five years, I was on staff at a large, nondenominational evangelical megachurch in New Jersey, just outside of New York City. The church was beautiful; the people were gorgeous souls, and the building was impeccably kept. You would walk in on a Sunday morning and think there is no happier, shinier place on earth, from the glint of strobe light off the metal drum set on the stage to the smile that was in every hug you got. Good people go to that church, and it was a place where I could fly my "Jesus freak" flag high and proud. Though I don't attend that church anymore for a multitude of reasons, Jesus is still my main man, and I am grateful for the time I spent in that environment.

Of course, nothing is always as it seems, and those shiny smiles and welcoming hugs hid a lot of pain—the pain of addictions, failing marriages, abuse, mental illness, you name it. A lot of people outside church critique it for its dysfunction, but for Pete's sake, *people* live in the church. Of course we're all hot messes. Of course we are imperfect. Just like the disciples—who often acted like pretty big jerks—we in the church have a very large capacity to be jerks. Some of us more than others, but still.

I do not wish to make light of the very real traumas that people have experienced at the hands of church authorities. Youth pastors raping their congregants, priests molesting little kids, and lead pastors harassing their staff for years and getting away with it are unconscionable realities that require justice. I have seen the system at work—and like the system that keeps the larger societal status quo happily humming along, the church's ecosystem is one that preferences silence, obedience, and a carefully controlled narrative at all times. I've seen abusive lead pastors practice extreme narcissism, and I've seen dysfunctional teams support them in these efforts. I've seen people—myself included—silenced for being too "divisive." I've watched talented, gifted women be relegated to phone work and refused the title of "pastor" despite their seminary degrees. I've seen dissenters be maligned in the public, congregational eye to protect the reputation of leaders. The system is broken, there is no doubt.

I've also seen immense grace pour out of church hearts like a soothing waterfall. I've seen the Holy Spirit work its way through hurt and pain like a healing oil finding its way to a wound. This is why I still hold out hope for the church. We have the beautiful Sophia of God, the maternal wisdom of the Holy Spirit, and she knows exactly how to kiss our brokenness and make us better. I do not mean this in a cute or flippant way. I mean that I have expectations of God and that I believe God will come through. I believe that there is a holy healing power that is nothing short of the divine maternal love of God and that this is the only thing that can save us from ourselves. Even from our whiteness.

Like everything else we're talking about, church is a paradox. Within that paradox can be found immense goodness—works around both charity and justice that change communities and people—and deep pain, such as the exclusion of women from leadership and the LGBTQIA community from, well, everything.

Underneath the everyday dysfunction and the shiny happy church hugs, there can be no refuting that there is a sinister history to the Christian tradition that can trace its lineage directly back to slavery and the origins of racism as we know it today. This is disappointing and gravely disturbing—but strangely, I believe church is where the hope is. Not church as it stands now—but a radically reimagined body of Christ that actually points to and emulates Jesus. As a Jesus freak myself (I've mostly stopped referring to myself as a Christian precisely because of the injustices perpetrated by the institution of Christianity), I do believe that the radical ways of Jesus—that Brown-skinned refugee from a "shithole" town in the Middle East—offer us a road to restoration and redemption.

But first, the church is called to do one very important, very Christian thing: *repent*. The Euro-American church has been the perpetrator of some grievous sins, and deep at the heart of them is racism. Collective lament and repentance are mandatory. We must be the ones to invite the Holy Spirit to kiss our wounds, urging us on to a corporate repentance that will lead the world into a new way of being.

The Most Evil Tithe

In his book *The Christian Imagination*, Willie James Jennings recounts the savage and disturbing moment when a slave trader's "cargo" disembarked from a ship in Portugal in 1444. Relayed through the words of Zurara, the chronicler of Prince Henry, an eyewitness to this horrific event, the retelling is stark and naked proof that actual humans—with all our full spectrum of emotions—were engaged with the horrors of the slave trade. Zurara described the Africans and their sorrow in detail. The great mourning, the wailing, the way mothers threw themselves on their young children when they realized they were going to be separated, regardless of the lashes they received. Fathers and sons torn apart, faces looking up at the sky, as if searching for God. Grief, wailing, fear, tears, horror. And Zurara? He saw this. He empathized with their pain. And *he prayed for them*.

Zurara the chronicler, the complicit slave trader, prayed for them.

He didn't ask for forgiveness. He asked God to give the Africans clarity and to alleviate their suffering, to offer them comfort because they didn't know what was going to happen to them next. In other words, he felt compassion—just not quite enough to stop what he was doing. He wrote, "It is not their religion but their humanity that maketh mine to weep in pity for their sufferings."[2] He went on to say to God that if animals understand the suffering of their own kind, "what wouldst Thou have my human nature to do on seeing before my eyes that miserable company, and remembering that they too are of the generation of the sons of Adam?" The man recognized their humanity—the savage construct had been replaced by the face of actual human beings—yet he did nothing to confront the system.

Zurara continued: "Following his deepest Christian instincts, [Prince Henry] ordered a tithe be given to God through the church. Two Black boys were given, one to the principal church in Lagos and another to the Franciscan convent on Cape Saint Vincent."

They gave two little boys—as a *fucking tithe*.

Don't you dare complain that I said the F-word here. If you're not more appalled by the idea that two precious little boys were given *as a tithe to the local church* than you are by my language, there's nothing I can say to you. If there was ever anything in the history of the world that deserves a nice, solid F-bomb, it's the idea that the holy body of Christ affirmed and accepted the institution of slavery to such a point that it accepted *children as tithes*. The whole idea of it is disgusting. So keep your language police home today, okay?

Of course, you and I—we would never do such a thing. If, like me, you're involved in any way in the world of Christendom, this idea probably sickens you, assuming you have gotten over my language and have let go of your pearls. If you're nonreligious, you might be feeling pretty relieved that you're not part of such a horrific practice. You might also be feeling a tad bit smug—after all, organized religion has always done evil things (except when it hasn't—but I'll get to that in a minute). But like immigrants who came to America long after slavery had ended, I don't want you nonreligious folk to feel like you're off the hook just yet. Because just like the more recent immigrant who can slide into the structures of whiteness, if you're white, you're benefiting from the same power systems as the rest of us. If you slid from the margins to the nice, bright center of whiteness, you have the church to thank.

Charity + Justice, Mercy + Missions

My last day in the big, shiny, contemporary evangelical church that I loved was the Sunday after the 2016 election. My church had once been called "the most diverse church ever" by an organization that studied such things, and it was true that on any given Sunday morning you could walk in and see Black people and white people, people in traditional African garb and people in Indian saris. In the lobby you would hear multiple languages being spoken—Spanish, French, and languages I could not recognize. The diversity was also generational and socioeconomic; for a time, while we were a storefront church, we had professional football players sitting next to homeless folk who came in from the cold. But we moved to a big, new building on a hill, far away from the downtown area, where the homeless could not reach. Eventually, those friends stopped coming. They left us to our shiny new existence.

Politically, the church was split. There were many of us who walked into church that Sunday morning after the election not just tired and disappointed. We walked in bereft. Here is the hardest thing for my heart to hold: the people who walked into that church that morning, who voted for a man I could never support, were people that I loved—deeply. Though it seems incomprehensible to me, I don't think those people could understand the deep fear and pain that election caused the other half of us. Based on my Facebook feed, it didn't seem as if they cared to try. Some of them, right there on Facebook, said I was going to hell for voting for Hillary Clinton in that election. Others of them will come to my page still to this day to debate my views while ignoring every other nonpolitical thing I post. These people I loved will police my political views and debate me on racial issues but will not congratulate my children on their accomplishments when I brag about them or laugh at my stupid cat memes.

That morning just days after the election, I went to church hoping for hope. I wanted to go there, to that shiny place, and find guidance for how to move forward in a world that seemed committed to evil things—a world that did not care for the poor or the homeless. A society that did not love our neighbor or welcome the stranger. A nation that did not care for racial justice or women or children. But that Sunday, I was profoundly disappointed. There was nothing I could find in that worship service about doing justice, loving mercy, and walking humbly with our God. In a brief, preworship commentary, the speaker played it safe, and I wanted something dangerous and bold, like Jesus. I wanted something as radical as the Beatitudes. What I got instead was "Some people really believe we have to follow the laws of the land; others really believe in welcoming the stranger. Both are accurate." Then it was business as usual. The worship band played, the big screens flashed, the feel-good sermon series about nothing related to what was happening in the world that day commenced.

I sobbed.

I could not go back. My church—the church I loved so deeply, that had cost me much and that I was so invested in that I would walk around straightening the children's art that hung in the hallways—was lukewarm and spit out (see Rev. 3:16). The fiery passion of the Jesus I knew from Scripture—the one who flipped the tables of empire and called out the religious leaders for being hypocrites—was not to be found there. Instead, the Jesus that lived there was tame and obedient, concerned with me having the shiny happy life of white America. This Jesus insisted that I be nice, be silent, and know my place. I wanted the dirty, blood-and-guts Jesus, the desert-walking Jesus who hung out with beggars and prostitutes out on the periphery, where things are known to get dicey.

I must be honest and say that my leaving was death by a million cuts, but this was by far the deadliest slice. I remember sobbing and being wrapped up in the arms of my best friend's mom, who sat in the row behind me. I knew it was my last time in that church. I was heartbroken. I also believed I was ruined for church forever.

The thing about it is this: my church was a church that loved charity but not justice. We loved our diversity, but diversity is not antiracism. In fact, like many organizations, we used our diversity as a marketing tool, consuming Black and Brown bodies by putting them front and center on our website, being sure to capture their images for the big screens, putting them on stage to demonstrate our wokeness. We made sure our staff was diverse, with people of color on the executive team and plenty of darker-hued faces on our printed materials, but we were never involved in actual justice work, because justice work is messy and requires bold confrontation of the status quo. That might be considered "divisive," and we were to avoid divisiveness at all costs.

We said we cared about the hungry and the homeless, and we did charity work—good, holy work—that would feed bellies and shelter the vulnerable, but we never did anything to challenge or change the systems that caused empty stomachs or generational poverty. We loved our do-good missions trips, because traveling to far-off places in Africa to build wells and hospitals made us feel like good people and even better Christians, but we never once questioned whether our own country's policies might be making those missions trips necessary, or whether we should maybe go to Africa to learn rather than to teach. We never once questioned whether our whiteness was a factor in why those Black people are poor.

We loved charity, because charity is easy and it makes us feel good about ourselves. Justice, on the other hand, is a long game.[3] It's hard and frustrating and sometimes overwhelming to the point of surrender. Justice work is by nature divisive, because there will always be people who want to maintain the status quo for what they have to lose. This is why Jesus said he did not come to bring peace. Jesus was probably one of the most divisive guys to ever walk the earth. But in modern-day churches, we love to talk about unity. And we choose so-called unity over justice any day of the week, because unity feels good, acts nice, and doesn't make a bit of difference to people who are suffering. "Unity" is just an ideological tool the white Christian empire uses to keep us all in our nice, timid places. Unity is about peacekeeping—doing anything necessary to keep things moving right along without disturbing whiteness. But Jesus was about peace-*making*—which is about making a peaceful world for *everyone*. And that means some of us have to get super uncomfortable for this Jesus kind of peace to happen.

But call me crazy, because I still have hope for the church.

Here Is Where the Hope Is

Happily for me, the church is full of rebels. It takes one to know one, and these are the folks who always catch my attention. As shameful as the embedded love affair between systemic racism and institutional church is, there can also be no doubt that for centuries there have been voices calling from the sacred desert, prophesying that Jesus was indeed an antiracist (as well as an LGBTQIA-affirming feminist radical—oh yes, I did). These voices come from Catholic and Protestant traditions alike, Black, white, Latinx, and Asian, male, female, and queer. They call for liberation and justice and point to the plethora of places in Scripture that say this is God's heart for humanity. These are the people who actually do justice, love mercy, and walk humbly with a God they believe is for all people, ready to show radical hospitality to all. These are the liberation theologians and the womanists, the radical priests and the Nuns on the Bus. They are the people that Jesus has gotten to—and damn it all if Jesus isn't really annoying about making us crazy uncomfortable until we can't take it anymore and we get up and *do* something.

This book—and my own antiracism work—would not be happening if it weren't for Jesus. Trust me when I tell you I would be way more comfortable living a quiet suburban life, posting cat memes to Instagram and grabbing a latte on my way to yoga.[4] But because I've encountered Jesus, he has taken hold of me and won't let me go. He requires much. I don't recommend him, unless you like to be radically changed. So don't go calling me an evangelical, like I'm trying to convert you or something. The last thing I suggest you do is follow Jesus, because the next thing you know, you'll be writing a book about racism and whiteness, when there was a time you couldn't even say the word *Black* in front of a Black person. Jesus is really annoying that way.

Repentance Road

At the risk of sounding like one of those sandwich-boarded, crazy-ass preachers you encounter on street corners in New York City who scream "Repent!" while they shake Bibles in the air, I'm here to tell you that the hope I have for the church is that we'll get serious about that key tenet of our faith—that pesky little repentance part. It's the part where we not only say we're sorry and ask for forgiveness, but we actually, like, *stop doing the thing we say we're sorry for* and become an agent of change in the world.

This is one of the things the church is supposed to be good at. Stories I've always heard in church say that the word *repent* comes from a military command for turning around, but this smacks of a patriarchal fascination with warfare, and I can't find any etymology to support the military part. The turning part, though—that's there. Repentance isn't just a penitent "Sorry." It means a radical turning from something sinful toward the heart of God. It is as much an action as it is a feeling. It is not just a *turning away* from, but a *moving to* something else. Which means all our good white guilt is nothing without some serious, solid action to back it up.

I believe the church needs to lead that action. We started this whole mess, and I believe we have the theology, the people, and the Holy Spirit to make it happen. But this hope of mine is a risk, because it will take bold leadership out of the mire of the status quo. It will take preachers—and I do mean white preachers leading white congregations—making bold statements and challenging their members to take a good, hard look at themselves. It will mean that these white leaders step down from their shiny platforms, take a seat, and learn from marginalized people: Black women, First Nations shamans, queer Latinx nonbinary trans refugees, Muslim hijab-wearing women. All bodies, in all their forms, need to be given voice in our churches. We need to stop assuming our own rightness, our own superiority, our own normalized standards of being. Churches need to open our tables and practice not just radical hospitality, but radical humility as well. In a profound act of submission to God's Holy Spirit, we need to lay down every aspect of our own power, authority, and moral justifications and trust that God can lead us out of this hell hole we've dug our white asses into—unless, of course, we don't really trust God.

Then we're all pretty much screwed.

Action Steps

Learn: What does your faith community (or the faith communities around you) do to combat racism, if anything?

Think: How are modern-day faith communities complicit in racism? In your understanding of God, how does God want faith communities to respond, collectively, to systemic racism?

Act: If necessary, be the one bold enough to speak out about racism—or the lack of antiracist activity—in your faith community.

Chapter Eleven

In Full Color

(Or, *Where We Go from Here*)

B eing a leader in the antiracism movement is a dance that is always contextual. There is no one specific step you can learn, no one type of music to move to. It is a daily becoming, relative to who is in the room and which dynamics are at play at any given time. It is the work of surrender, of answering the quiet whisper of that strange Holy Spirit. This makes the work dangerous. It does not make the work unnecessary.

The antiracism movement needs white leaders—people who are pointing out whiteness at every turn and helping other white people to see it too. But what that looks like changes daily. I certainly don't mean that we should continue to take power from the BIPOC community. Rather, I mean that white people need to lead other white people through this journey of dismantling and unpacking our pseudosupremacy and all the ways it manifests in the world. Sometimes this will mean modeling boldness, speaking out when it's terrifying, protesting, risking arrest, and losing friends and family members. Other times it will require us to take a seat, to dim our own light a bit so as not to diffuse the lights of others. That takes some humility, but good people don't worry about not being noticed. Good people worry about whether the light they emanate offers value to the world. If you have a light you want to be all bright and shiny, make damn sure it's an antiracist light before you flip the switch.

Hopefully, this "going first" means that as white people we are in such deep relationship with people who are different from us that we can tell with just the catch of an eye or a shift of energy what they need from us at any given time—if they need anything at all. Being a white leader in the antiracist movement is all about learning how to read rooms. It's about noticing what's happening and being willing to recognize that we may not be capable of noticing it at all. It's about cultivating a type of humility we've never embodied before. It's about serving the world and healing ourselves from our own racism.

This will be an entirely painful process. It will not be easy or even simple, and it will have no nice, clean ending. It will be an ongoing, never-ending work of painful self-examination. Worse, we must face the fact that this examination will absolutely result in some horrible self-discoveries. It's a painful thing to realize that we're not as good as we thought we were. It's a realization that leaves emotional scars, but those scars become a map right there on our skin to a better, more just way of being in the world.

Unpacking our inherent racism is a pretty gruesome process, and our defensiveness is a deep, neurobiological process that has dug trenches in our brains. It is tribal and emotional and is bound to our most basic biological needs for safety. This does not make it right or just; it only makes it powerful. No wonder it's hard to comprehend. No wonder it's difficult work and dangerous to unpack. We must practice agency over it—over these fears and these deep-seeded untruths. It is painful stuff, this discovery that we may, indeed, be racists. We get to mourn that fact. Mourning is good, because it leads to lament, and lament leads to repentance.

But what we don't get to do is use this pain as an excuse to not engage in the work—or even worse, to get some sort of props for a job well done. Good people don't ask for credit for being good. Truly good people just do the right thing because it's the right thing. So as we engage in our antiracism work, we get to have our feelings, but we also get to process our feelings carefully and only in the right company, in the right spaces. We don't get to go online and defend our goodness or our mourning to the BIPOC community. They're smart enough to figure out on their own if we're safe. They've been doing that for ages, and we might not be as safe for them as we thought anyways. We don't get to have the spotlight shine on us for being good white people. What we get to do is shine the spotlight where it has never shone before—on the beautiful array of colorful faces who have something hard and beautiful to teach us about ourselves.

We get to do the hard work of repentance, of not simply turning away from our own stagnant desire for the status quo, but actively moving toward a creation that is more just for all people. That is our labor in this beloved community; that is our hammer and nail, our wooden boards and concrete floors. We get to walk through the mire of our own making, to scrub that muck off our boots, and to build something new. This is our sweat equity, the work of our scuffed and dirty hands. It is ugly but worthy work.

We also get to show other white people how to do the same, and that work will not always be glorious. It will involve ruined family dinners and tense conversations with coworkers. It will be lost friendships and online arguments and a boatload of mistake-induced self-doubt. That is the cost of this awakening, of this allyship. As white people, we've been getting a free ride for a long, long time. Now it's time we pay our dues.

White Awakening and the Stages of Grief

It's easy to demonize people who resist their own racial awakening. I have been both the person resisting and the person rolling her eyes at someone who doesn't seem to get it. Now, though, I realize that as much as I'd just like to write these people off as heels, the truth is far more complex. As I have prayed about it and thought about it and tried hard to listen, I have realized that we're not just being jerks when we get defensive or angry at being called out for our racist tendencies. We're mourning. Our white identity is dying, and we are moving through the stages of grief that are often associated with losing a loved one.

According to the website Grief.com, the five stages of grief are denial, anger, bargaining, depression, and acceptance. A sixth possible stage has recently been identified: finding meaning. As we unpack some of the ways white people respond when we are confronted with our own whiteness and our complicity in a racist system, we can see how these different stages operate in our psyches. This process is not linear. It's messy and complicated, and sometimes people get stuck in one difficult place. But if we are aware of how we are moving through these stages from a racial perspective, then we can have more patience and awareness for ourselves, as well as more compassion for people who are just beginning the process. Let's now take a look at each stage from its racialized perspective.

Denial

In this first stage, white people who have been confronted with their own racism will often have a strong, almost knee-jerk reaction, and they will be unable to see why or how their behavior or their words were racist. They will often place blame on the person who called out their behavior, telling that person to "not be so sensitive," to "calm down," and they will vehemently oppose any logical explanations around why they are complicit in a racist society. This stage will often include explanations about how they have many relationships with people of color, so they can't possibly be racist. If they do, indeed, have friends of color, they will seek affirmation from them during this stage. If they don't, they will seek affirmation from their other white friends, retelling the story to demonstrate how they are totally not racist. (Many of these defensive strategies are discussed in chapter 3.)

Denial is an understandable emotion when you're being confronted with an ugly truth about yourself. It's natural to want to insist on your own goodness and to believe that the world is inherently good as well. It's not fun to realize that you are part of a world that is unsafe for huge amounts of people. Good people like you and me are rightfully bothered by this truth and would prefer that it wasn't true. Denial offers us a grace period, a time to get used to an idea that's extremely difficult for the human psyche to accept.

Anger

Anger often comes right on the heels of denial. As they think about the situation, good white racists will begin to get angry not just at the person who first confronted them, but at any person who represents a threat to the status quo. Here's where you will find angry refusals to acknowledge how race may be at play in news stories or policy. It will take center stage in any racialized conversation and will often intimidate people who may be trying to point out racist behavior. This type of white anger can often be toxic and centered in spaces in which people of color exist, but just as often it is internalized and quietly nurtured, only to emerge later as a strange kind of bitterness, or a desire for retribution—like calling the police in a "while Black" situation.

Bargaining

We see racial bargaining every time justifications are made for racist behavior or racist events are explained away. When the unarmed young man is shot in the back by police, we are told, "If only he hadn't run away," rather than, "If only that cop had been better trained and not quite so racist." When a woman discusses a workplace microaggression, the good white racist will say, "Your coworker probably didn't mean it that way—you're just being oversensitive," rather than, "Wow, that sounds exhausting. Are you okay?"

In a racialized context, bargaining helps maintain the status quo by allowing us to think that maybe it's not as bad as it seems. It keeps us comfortable and able to maintain our own denial while at the same time feeling like we're being supportive or offering an intelligent critique of a situation.

Depression

It simply doesn't feel good to recognize that you've done harm to another person, especially when that's the last thing you intended. It's even worse if that person is someone you love and care about.

There is also that strange, psychic borderland between our denial of reality and the racial truth, and that's where depression kicks in. It's partly about the realization that you are responsible for doing something you're not proud of. It's partly because it's just not fun to be called out, and it's awkward to admit your own mistake. But it's also because when you think about the whole, big thing, it seems impossible. It seems too big. There is nothing you can do about it anyway, it seems. As white people awaken to the fact that we are complicit in an evil that we have little individual control over, something in us breaks a little. A feeling of helplessness overcomes us, and it's hard to find a hope that matters in this stage. This is, I think, that place we've all been pushing against, the emotion we did not want to experience, that depth to which we did not want to go. It's looking our own self square in the eye and realizing we don't like everything we see.

Acceptance

In a racialized context, the acceptance stage is when the work begins. It's when a white person may start to independently study race and racism, listening to and reading voices of color, and openly making mistakes. This is the time good white racists may begin to understand that while they have been complicit in racist systems, they also have agency over their responses. They begin to find their voice and will slowly begin to speak out against racist policy in their politics and racist jokes at their dinner table. It is the beginning of a lifelong process of unearthing their own racist thought patterns and of recognizing the way race plays out in the systems and institutions in which we partake.

Finding Meaning

In this final stage, we begin to forge a new way forward while acknowledging the pain of our racialized past. This is no Pollyanna color-blindness. Rather, this is an opportunity for lament and restoration, for true healing through reparations. Here is where the real transformation is, as white people begin to reimagine a new way to be white in the world and work to make that new way a reality. This is the place supremacy is rendered useless, privilege is no longer hoarded, and true equity is the goal. It is not clean-cut and easy to find; it is becoming and being created, the intangible future for which we work. Individually, good white racists find meaning by participating in this work, even if it does not come to fruition in their lifetime.

What We Have to Do: Three Levels of True Antiracism Work

If we understand now that America is, essentially, a paradox, built on an amazing idea that we've never lived up to—that all people are created equal—while at the same time being also an inherently racist community built on an idea that the white people who stole the land from the original inhabitants were somehow superior, then today we have to make a choice. We must decide which of these truths we want to bring us into the future. We have to ask ourselves whether we are going to believe the truth in the founding documents or are going to decide to lean into our racist underpinnings, that deep well of hatred. I believe we are capable of creating an experiment. It will not be easy or simple. It will be messy and hard and probably really ugly. But we need to make the decision and then act on it. This action needs to occur on three levels: personal, interpersonal, and collective.

Unpacking racism requires both introspection and action—a radical self-awareness and a willingness to move into a new space. As we live into a new way to be white in the world, as we work to dismantle our sickened social constructs and rebuild a healthy, moral whiteness, we will move through a nonlinear process of inner and outer work, of mistakes, backslides, and spirals of new layers of yet more work to be done.

Personal

The personal work is often sparked by a conversation or an event—perhaps even a book like this—that strikes a discord in your soul. On the one hand, you want to rage against it, while on the other, you sense the truth there, on the periphery of your defensiveness. Indeed, defensiveness is often a sign that truth is hovering. Otherwise, why would we care? If it had nothing to do with us, we could just walk away. Defensiveness is our first sign that there's something there we need to look at.

This personal work is nuanced and complex and will reveal itself over time, and in the most inconvenient places. You will be confronted with it when you least expect it, but once you become aware of your own racist tendencies, you will start to notice them more often. It takes a deep and wise soul to question one's own assumptions and automatic thoughts. Not everyone is willing. It takes good people to do this hard work—people like you and me. I've been hard on you in this book, and with good reason. But you're a good person, and you're up for this task. I believe in you. I believe in us. I have to, because knowing what I now know about my own whiteness, if I didn't believe in us a little bit, I might not be able to get up in the morning and face all the hatred in the world, knowing all the dangers those people I love who walk around in Black or Brown bodies face every day.

Interpersonal

The interpersonal is a borderland. It is a place of practice, but it can also be a place of malpractice. We must be so careful here, friends—so very careful. These are souls and bodies we are deal-ing with—our own and those of others. The interpersonal racial space is where we can enter into the practice of allyship and learn its subtle dances. If you do not have any friends from the BIPOC community, this may be hard. So your first step is to enter into the paradox of intentionally seeking relationship with people of color without making the mistake of tokenizing them and just searching for your new Black friend. This is a long-haul game. This is about investing in real relationship. You probably don't know where to start. Here is where the spiritual practice comes in: get on your knees and pray, or get on your pillow and meditate. Work with healthy intention here, but infuse it with humility.

This interpersonal space is where we learn how our whiteness acts in our relationships with people of color, and how we can practice agency over it. It is the space where the personal and the interpersonal interact and collide—for it will be malpractice if you expect the people of color in your space to educate you. That is not the point of your relationship with them. The point of your relationship is, well, *relationship*. In authentic relationships—and those take time and energy—you can learn how to give honor and emotional space and to receive hard truths about yourself. These are the most sacred of relationships. Cherish them.

The interpersonal space is also the borderland of the white empire, and you are the rebel force of resistance. This is a dangerous space, and your mouth might go dry here; your tongue might swell in fear. These are the dining-room table spaces, the emails that go back and forth between parents and children; these are the public, third spaces where you encounter a racist barista exercising pseudosupremacy and you are the one white ally to a stranger in the room. This is the space where you bring your personal learnings into relationship with others, and some of those others may not like it one bit. This is where you have much to lose from your personal sphere, and where you must make different choices than what your safety-oriented brain is telling you. This is stepping out of your comfort zone, widening it to include the labor of peacemaking. And remember: peacemaking is not peacekeeping. You know when you are keeping the peace because you'll be nice and comfortable. If you're peace*making*, a whole lot of stuff might be going to shit around you, and the last thing you'll feel is safe.

Collective

The collective is where the activism is. This is raising your voice along with the voices of others through your vote, through protest, through the work of your hands in the world. The collective antiracist work is where social organizing happens, where you work to unify both people and money for power to resist oppressive systems. Trust me when I tell you that oppressive regimes are very well organized. Collective white, antiracist work must become so as well. We need white leaders to lead other white people through the work of personal, interpersonal, and collective antiracism work, and white leaders need to submit to leaders of color to learn how to do that well. As white people working in the public sphere, if we are not willing to take leadership from people of color, than we cannot come anywhere close to calling ourselves truly antiracist—because in that case, we're just not.

The collective white work must also be about reconstructing our identities as white people. I long for a day when we might no longer refer to racial categories, but I know this is somewhat Pollyannaish of me. So if race is here to stay as a social construct, I want us to make whiteness new. I want us to reclaim this so-called "white pride" and give us something to actually be proud of. The bastards who took our identity and made it about supremacy—and continue to do so today—need to step down. We need to take back our whiteness and make it about service, humility, and a holistic, healthy identity. This is a call for white people to start being angry and vocal about how our identity has been used to manipulate us with dangling carrots of privilege and pseudosupremacy. This is a call for all of us to wake up to that in which we have participated and repent so that we can deconstruct the systems of oppression in which we all participate. I am both solidly cynical about this possibility and radically hopeful, in a very Jesus-y sort of way. Like everything else, my hope is a paradox.

Action Steps

The coach in me wants to provide us all with a new vision, a new way to lean into our whiteness, but I confess that I don't have the fullness of imagination for it. I have some imagination, and ideas hover there, just out of reach. We need to do this together. I want to give us some ideas—some that I am pulling from the periphery of my imagination and others that I am simply supporting here—that can help us envision a way forward. I encourage you to come up with your own. Send me an email—seriously. We have to do this work together. So if you have an idea that I don't cover here, hit me up. Meanwhile, here are some ideas to start off with.

1. Publicly and vocally support economic reparations. The value of the labor an enslaved person generated would equate to anywhere between $50,000 and $150,000 annually today.[1] The restoration of this kind of wealth to the descendants of slaves would allow for things like homeownership, investments, and education, things that were stolen from enslaved people and their descendants. These are literal fruits of labor that were stolen from enslaved people and redistributed into the white empire's economy for the benefit of white people.

This does not include the value of land and other properties stolen from BIPOC communities throughout the history of the United States. It does not include the higher costs paid for mortgages for houses in redlined neighborhoods. It does not account for the lost wages due to mass incarceration and the undereducation of whole categories of people. It does not include the wages and productivity lost due to the effects of generational trauma and abuse. It certainly does not include the dollars that would have been generated for their own families by all those precious lives lost. If we're going to look at it from a purely economic standpoint, much is owed to both the indigenous populations from whom land was stolen and to the enslaved people from whom labor was stolen.

But nothing stokes the fear of white people—especially poor white people—more than the idea of economic reparations. It's as if we are going to be made to personally write a check out of our meager bank accounts to a stereotyped trope, some "welfare queen" or "gang member" who will misuse the funds for which we toiled so diligently. This is a fallacy of epic proportions, a misconception that needs to be corrected immediately.

Here in gilded America, we love to venerate our millionaires and billionaires, as if they are evidence of the fact of our goodness. *If they made it, so can we.* And I do not deny anyone their millions. I'm a sucker for a good rags-to-riches story like anyone else. But I do have a problem with a person having enough money to, for example, pay off the school loans of an entire graduating class without even blinking an eye, while systemic obstacles still keep the majority of people—mostly BIPOC communities—poor. At what point does all this accumulation become enough? What is that doing to our souls?

Simple tax plans that focus on the ultrawealthy could do more than enough to fund a healthy reparations program, and that reparations program can be much more creative than just a check in the mail. It can revolve around wealth-building programs focused on homeownership and education, for example. Much has been written about these proposals in other places, and I encourage you to read them. I encourage you to use your good, brilliant mind to come up with your own ideas. I encourage you to harass your representatives to support reparations, and I encourage you to vocalize your support around your holiday dinner tables and educate your skin kin on why reparations are necessary.

2. Enter into the practice of emotional reparations. One of the key ways white people demonstrate our defensiveness in racial conversations is to claim we did not mean harm. Now that we understand that very often our good intentions are less important than the actual harm we've done, we can take responsibility for the result of our actions. Financial reparations are important, but just as important, I believe, is to make sure that people in the BIPOC community feel as if they have been heard, seen, and understood.

This needs to play out on the national level with a real truth and reparations effort. A large, long-term event in which our nation spends serious time listening to the real stories of families who have been harmed by the slave trade and its insidious, generational abuses ever since is imperative, as is a period of national lament. Every year, the names of the victims of 9/11 are read aloud on the anniversary of that horrible day. Meanwhile, our country is responsible for some of the most evil, vile, and long-term human rights violations, and we have never once even uttered a semblance of an apology. The two populations who most deserve this moment in history—and forever more to be remembered—are African Americans and First Nations people. Supporting a truth and reconciliation effort is redemptive work that white people can engage in on the collective level of antiracism labor.

But you and I, it might seem, are not in a position to make this kind of thing happen. Still, we can enter into the sacred practice of emotional reparations every time we interact with the BIPOC community in person or online. So often I hear white people bemoaning the fact that they are being treated unfairly by people of color because of some racial mistake they made, and can't people realize that their intentions were good? But rarely do we as white people want to give the BIPOC community the same emotional space to process their own racial experiences.

We want people who have experienced grave injustice to be polite about expressing their grief and their rage. We take it personally and get defensive or disappear when their emotions become too much for us to bear. This is a cop-out. Though it may feel uncomfortable at the time, offering emotional reparations—even if it just means staying in the room while someone expresses intense emotions that are both completely about us and not about us at all—is important, sacred, and redemptive work.

I confess that I struggle with this. I was lurking once in an online conversation in which a diverse community was discussing whether white women should develop "safe spaces" in which to unpack our racist baggage. Black women in the group were expressing their dismay at this language, and I admit that I, too, was uncomfortable with it, because generally speaking, white women are pretty safe racially. Naming this online community a "safe space" indicated that white people were the ones being victimized, and it put us in the center. Another white woman gave words to what I'd been thinking when she offered that what we really mean by "safe space" is a place where we as white women can unpack our privilege and racist tendencies without doing further harm to our BIPOC siblings. That's important to me, but if I'm going to be honest, so is saving face. In other words, creating "safe spaces" for white people is about keeping our assholery to ourselves so that we don't continue to hurt people, but also so that we don't come off looking so bad.

A Black woman in the group said, "No. You don't get off so easy. I want to see your discomfort. I want to see you squirm. It feels like reparations."

This made me uncomfortable, because I am always dancing on the line between what is a form of healthy emotional reparation and what is abusive. This felt like it bordered on abusive. I asked my friend Ben Tapper, who is an expert in radical self-awareness, for his thoughts. He said, "When I hear someone say they want to see white women squirm, what I hear them saying is that they want white people to have some skin in the game. They don't want white people to be able to just do all their ugly work in private and then be the good woke person in public. They want to know these women have done the work." That made sense to me. It doesn't make me more comfortable. But it does make sense. Because when it comes to emotional reparations, my comfort is not the point.

3. Practice active learning. We spent an entire chapter talking about the power of language, and I think it's an excellent place to start this work. As we listen to the ways our country talks about race, we can both learn and unlearn; we can recognize and call out, and then we can reimagine new ways of speaking about ourselves and about race in general. As we do this imagining, we can construct new language that deconstructs hierarchy and leans into paradox, the and/and of things.

It is imperative that white people self-educate. We can no longer go through the world blissfully unaware of our inherent racism, insisting all the while on our goodness. This is to our detriment and to the detriment of others. It is a lie. It is time for us to do the reading, engage the work, lean into the hard conversations, stay in the room, and force our imaginations to think bigger, better things. Yeah, it's tough, but good people stick it out when things get tough. Good people stay in the room. We do our own work. We own up to our mistakes. We reevaluate and reimagine. We learn, we get better, we make amends.

4. Deconstruct "diversity efforts." As we begin to understand the subtle dynamics of the way racism plays out in relationship and in space, it becomes imperative that we also begin to reimagine diversity efforts. Diversity efforts are often more an exercise in making white people feel good about being "not racist," and in fact, they often prop up the status quo by requiring assimilation on the part of people in the BIPOC community.

Too often, so-called "diverse" spaces are really just rich, fertile ground for color-blind racism, where all the white people can pretend whiteness isn't a thing and all the people of color can fit in really nicely as long as they don't try to "make it all about race."

The problem with diversity efforts and their resulting assimilation is that for all the ways they appear to be celebrating difference, they are actually more about highlighting commonality. This seems like it would be a great thing—hey, we've got more in common than what we don't, and that's awesome, right?

Well, sure. But also, no.

When we only focus on our sameness, we start believing that sameness is the norm to which we all need to aspire, and it's a pretty sure bet that the norm to which everyone will be expected to aspire is the dominant identity: whiteness. I think the next step in creating a truly antiracist world must include a real celebration of difference. I don't believe that difference is a thing to be overcome through integration and diversity efforts. Instead of facing difference with fear, judgment, and the certainty of our own rightness, I believe we can come to the table of God with curiosity and a deep longing for what the divine hopes to reveal about itself through the difference sitting across the table from us. If God is a diamond, let us see each holy facet for its own beauty—without trying to make it look like ours.

Of course, this type of effort must come with incredible humility, which is something we good white racists really need to work on. We come packing a brittle white ego almost everywhere we go, and it keeps us too fragile to enter into the discomfort of humility. When Jesus practiced humility, it pissed people off. Where they wanted a king, Jesus brought them a lamb. This type of humility recognizes that not all spaces need or welcome our whiteness. A true diversity program understands that there are some places where we just don't get to go. Rather than being hyperfocused on creating spaces where everyone assimilates into the white way of doing things, white people need to just be cool that Black spaces, Latinx spaces, indigenous spaces, and Japanese spaces exist, and let them be. There is, after all, a time to come together and a time to stay apart. True diversity allows for both of these experiences.

To reimagine diversity efforts, we need to start with our education programs. We need to begin dismantling not just power structures in education but also what we teach and how we teach it. Who teaches it is equally important; there needs to be a huge collective effort to recruit members of the BIPOC community—in all of its diversity—into teaching and education administration. While we're at it, we should probably take a good, hard look at our history curriculums too. Our teaching methods should be reevaluated to allow for an examination of unconscious bias and critical thinking from the get-go. I don't want to hear how little kids are incapable of critical thinking. If my eleven-year-old son can question whether something is racist or not, I'm pretty sure other eleven-year-olds can too.

The way we carry out scientific research—including within the social sciences—needs to be rehauled as well. I often wonder how our capitalistic and colonizing mindsets have caused us to miss incredible contributions from indigenous populations that would benefit the entire world, white people included. I wonder about a possible cure for cancer in a shaman's plants that we have trampled on, dug up in our quest for gold, or allowed Big Pharma to hide so it can sell us a tiny, plasticized pill. I wonder whether the mind that might be able to save our planet from global warming isn't living a life of poverty, with education and other resources unavailable to her because of the color of her skin.

Of course, diversity must be reimagined in our politics and judicial system—and in this, I believe we may be on our way. A truly diverse government that accurately reflects the diversity of our people is the way all the rest will change. It is only when members of oppressed communities actually receive their fair share of power that anything will actually begin to change, and if we, as white people, really want to be good, it's our job to stop standing in the way of this important change. In fact, it is our responsibility to help this change happen with our votes, our donations, and our advocacy.

New Imaginations

Being antiracist is good and right. I want to be against racism. But I also want to be for something, and I think we need to collectively reimagine what that could be. I am for the idea of the Beloved Community—that gorgeous idea Martin Luther King Jr. made popular during the civil rights movement. This Beloved Community is, according to the King Center,

> a global vision, in which all people can share in the wealth of the earth. In the Beloved Community, poverty, hunger and homelessness will not be tolerated because international standards of human decency will not allow it. Racism and all forms of discrimination, bigotry and prejudice will be replaced by an all-inclusive spirit of sisterhood and brotherhood. In the Beloved Community, international disputes will be resolved by peaceful conflict-resolution and reconciliation of adversaries, instead of military power. Love and trust will triumph over fear and hatred. Peace with justice will prevail over war and military conflict.[2]

The cynic in me looks at how far America has fallen from this ideal. But the radical hope in me insists that we have what it takes. Just some good old American grit should do the job. Like the child I once was who waved her little flag on a stick and believed she lived in the best country in the world, I want to believe that American values can lead the way to the Beloved Community. If they don't, I want to believe that Americans are good enough and gritty enough to scrap them all and start from scratch.

I also believe in God. I believe Jesus was a manifestation of God on earth and that Jesus shows us everything we need to know. Jesus wasn't exactly tame, or nice, or polite. He was passionate and weepy; he was strange and outspoken. He was the embodiment of the Beloved Community, with his open tables of radical welcome and all that loving people stuff. Jesus can show America the way, if only America would stop trying to insist that Jesus is a white American.

I also believe in our inherent goodness—yours and mine. This is a stubborn hope borne of no evidence other than that we are made in God's image, so God's got to be in there somewhere. With that indwelling God—a God who parts seas and heals bodies and resurrects the dead—I believe that our humanity can be resurrected too. I believe that the power of radical love can be so transformational that it can both convict and restore; it can restrain our dominant ego, and it can send us out into the world to lead us to a new way. This book is a manifesto for white people to start doing better, because I believe we actually can. It's time for us to rise up and fight to get our own identity back. Not the identity that has been steeped in privilege and used as a tool for evil, but rather a white identity of which we can actually be proud. This is not a paternalistic altruism but rather a humble heart of service, a rich understanding of our own cultural heritage, and a recognition and ownership of our own mistakes.

I believe in this beautiful image, and so I have to ask, what is my part in creating it? Who do I have to be as a white person to make this vision come true? Who do I need to ask you to be as we move into community together? This is where our new imaginings need to happen. This is generational work, in which we intentionally leave our children with a more holistic view of themselves and our world than we were given. I want to be my whole self on this earth—the whole self I was created to be, not the self that whiteness made. I want to discard that self for something more beautiful, more generous, and less fearful and greedy. I want to live into this Beloved Community, and to be a person who creates it wherever I go. I want to set the big Jesus table, and throw wide open the doors to the banquet hall.

But there's a catch: I need you to imagine with me.

I need you to help me be the good person I like to think I am. Let's be good together. To do this, we have to be willing to be uncomfortable for a bit. We have to stretch our vision and our imagination and do the mental labor, the emotional excavation, and the psychic explorations to root out every seed of racist thought and supremacist ideology. We need to be brave and to call out, to speak up, to raise our voices and lower our false pride.

We need to show up online and at the voting booth. We need to show up at protests and town hall meetings. As white people, we need to use our privilege to do good in the world.

Most likely, if you've read this far, you already have a heart for this work. Now the job is twofold. We have to keep learning, and we have to share what we've learned with other white people. Not all of them will be ready, and that's okay. Keep talking. Very often, when I've entered into conversations online with people who seem determined to miss the point, friends ask me why I bother. I tell them it's for the people who are watching. In some cases, those are BIPOC people who are tired, who don't want to do this emotional labor anymore and honestly shouldn't have to. But more importantly, it's for white people who are watching— and learning how to confront their own racism and that of others.

The point is, I believe in them, and I believe in you. Let's let goodness reign in the world and in our hearts. But for that to happen, we have work to do. This is serious business. It will take imagination and steadfastness and courage and boldness and education. And we can't wait for another day or another time. We have to start right now—you and me. We have to start being good. *Now.*

Because the time is urgent.

People are dying.

Notes

Foreword

1. "A Call for Unity," Stanford Web Archive Portal, Stanford University Libraries, https://swap.stanford.edu/20141218230016/http://mlk-kpp01.stanford.edu/kingweb/popular_requests/frequentdocs/clergy.pdf.
2. Dr. Martin Luther King, Jr., "Letter from a Birmingham Jail," University of Pennsylvania African Studies Center, https://www.africa.upenn.edu/Articles_Gen/Letter_Birmingham.html.
3. King, Jr., "Letter from a Birmingham Jail."

Introduction

1. For more information about the Take a Knee Movement, see https://www.sbnation.com/2016/9/11/12869726/colin-kaepernick-national-anthem-protest-seahawks-brandon-marshall-nfl.

Chapter 1: The Good Nation of America

1. Our American narrative rarely includes just how much Russia had to do with the Allied victory in World War II, preferring to maintain our heroship. Just sayin'.
2. It's possible that this famous photo depicts a sexual assault. Google it.
3. I first heard the phrase "a place where everyone has enough and no one needs to be afraid" from Tim Conder in a class he taught on social organizing.
4. Lloyd Marcus, "A Case for America's Goodness," *American Thinker*, June 16, 2018, https://www.americanthinker.com/articles/2018/06/a_case_for_americas_goodness.html.
5. James Dobson, "Dr. Dobson's Visit to the Border," July 2019, https://drjamesdobson.org/about/july-newsletter-2019.

6. Adrian F. Ward, "Scientists Probe Human Nature—and Discover We Are Good, After All," *Scientific American*, November 20, 2012, https://www .scientificamerican.com/article/scientists-probe-human-nature-and-discover -we-are-good-after-all/.

7. Kirwan Institute for the Study of Race and Ethnicity, *State of the Science: Implicit Bias Review 2017* (Columbus: Ohio State University, 2017), 10.

Chapter 2: The White Empire

1. David G. Horrell, *Ecological Hermeneutics: Biblical, Historical, and Theological Perspectives* (London: T&T Clark, 2010), chapter 10.

2. Philip L. Berg, "Racism and the Puritan Mind," *Phylon* 36 (March 1975): 2–3, https://eric.ed.gov/?id=ej116852.

3. Matthew Frye Jacobson, *Whiteness of a Different Color: European Immigrants and the Alchemy of Race* (Cambridge, MA: Harvard University Press, 1999), 7.

4. Kirwan Institute for the Study of Race and Ethnicity, *State of the Science: Implicit Bias Review 2016* (Columbus: Ohio State University, 2016), 15.

5. Kirwan Institute, *State of the Science*, section 2.1.

6. Kirwan Institute, section 2.1.

7. Thandeka, *Learning to Be White: Money, Race, and God in America* (New York: Continuum, 1999), 12.

8. Kirwan Institute, *State of the Science*, 15.

Chapter 3: Gaslit and Ghosted

1. A term drawn from the movie *Gaslight*, gaslighting refers to a psychological phenomenon in which one person causes another to question their perception of reality through subtle lies and manipulation.

2. Angelique M. Davis and Rose Ernst, "Racial Gaslighting: Politics, Groups, and Identities," *ResearchGate*, November 23, 2017, 3, https://www.researchgate .net/publication/321253827_Racial_gaslighting/citation/download.

3. Davis and Ernst, "Racial Gaslighting," 2–3.

4. Tuesda Roberts and Dorinda J. Carter Andrews, "A Critical Race Analysis of the Gaslighting against African American Teachers: Considerations for Recruitment and Retention," in *Contesting the Myth of a "Post Racial Era": The Continued Significance of Race in U.S. Education*, ed. Dorinda J. Carter Andrews and Franklin Tuitt (New York: Peter R. Lang, 2013), 78.

5. Dacher Keltner and Jeremy Adam Smith, "The Psychology of Taking a Knee" (blog post), *Scientific American*, September 29, 2017, https://blogs.scien tificamerican.com/voices/the-psychology-of-taking-a-knee/.

6. *Twelve Steps and Twelve Traditions* (New York: Alcoholics Anonymous World Services, 1981), 42.

Chapter 4: The Power of Language

1. Teresa Godwin Phelps, *Shattered Voices: Language, Violence, and the Work of Truth Commissions* (Philadelphia: University of Pennsylvania Press, 2004), 40.

2. Phelps, *Shattered Voices*, 43.
3. Phelps, *Shattered Voices*, 43.
4. Linguist Max Weinreich once said, "A language is a dialect with an army or a navy." While most linguists consider AAVE to be a dialect of Standard American English, other scholars believe it deserves to be its own language because of the way it has been influenced by indigenous African languages. However, systemic and linguistic racism prevent it from being regarded in the United States as its own language.
5. Maya Lewis, "As a Black Woman, I Wish I Could Stop Code-Switching. Here's Why," *Everyday Feminism*, April 23, 2018, https://everydayfeminism .com/2018/04/stop-code-switching/.
6. Phelps, *Shattered Voices*, 50.

Chapter 5: The Mis-Education of America

1. Brian McCadden, "Why Is Michael Always Getting Timed Out?" in *Classroom Discipline in American Schools: Problems and Possibilities for Democratic Education*, ed. Ronald E. and Barbara McEwan Landau Butchart (Albany, NY: State University of New York Press, 1998), 124.
2. Kim Cary Warren, *The Quest for Citizenship: African American and Native American Education in Kansas, 1880–1935* (Chapel Hill: University of North Carolina Press, 2010), 23.
3. Warren, *Quest for Citizenship*, 22.
4. Angelina Castagno, *Educated in Whiteness: Good Intentions and Diversity in Schools* (Minneapolis: University of Minnesota Press, 2014), 26.
5. David M. Ramey, "The Social Structure of Criminalized and Medicalized School Discipline," *Sociology of Education*, July 2015, 181–201.

Chapter 6: Justifying Ourselves

1. Thomas J. Pressly, "'The Known World' of Free Black Slaveholders: A Research Note on the Scholarship of Carter G. Woodson," *Journal of African American History* 91 (winter 2006): 81–87.
2. Angela Hanks, Danyelle Solomon, and Christian E. Weller, "Systematic Inequality: How America's Structural Racism Helped Create the Black-White Wealth Gap," Center for American Progress, February 21, 2018, https://www.americanprogress.org/issues/race/reports/2018/02/21/447051 /systematic-inequality/.
3. Hanks et al., "Systematic Inequality."
4. Erika Harrell, "Black Victims of Violent Crime," Bureau of Justice Statistics Special Report (Washington, DC: Office of Justice Programs, 2007), table 2.
5. Mark Follman, Gavin Anderson, and Deanna Pan, "US Mass Shootings, 1982–2019: Data from Mother Jones' Investigation," MotherJones.com, February 15, 2019, https://www.motherjones.com/politics/2012/12/mass -shootings-mother-jones-full-data/.
6. Geneive Abdo, "Like Most Americans, U.S. Muslims Concerned about Extremism in the Name of Islam," Pew Research Center, August 14, 2017,

https://www.pewresearch.org/fact-tank/2017/08/14/like-most-americans-u-s
-muslims-concerned-about-extremism-in-the-name-of-islam/.

Chapter 7: White People's Posse

1. Charles W. Mills, *The Racial Contract* (Ithaca, NY: Cornell University Press, 1997), 10–11.
2. Mills, *Racial Contract*, 12.
3. Mills, 11–13.
4. Mills, 17–18.
5. Mills.
6. For more information about this incident, see Darran Simon, "Police Release 911 Call in Arrest of Black Starbucks Customers," CNN.com, April 17, 2018, https://www.cnn.com/2018/04/17/us/philadelphia-starbucks-911-call/index .html.

Chapter 8: Unequal Justice

1. Angela Hattery and Earl Smith, *Policing Black Bodies: How Black Lives Are Surveilled and How to Work for Change*, Kindle version (Lanham, MD: Rowman & Littlefield, 2018), loc 389.
2. Statistics from https://mappingpoliceviolence.org/.
3. Ashley Nellis, "The Color of Justice: Racial and Ethnic Disparity in State Prisons," The Sentencing Project, June 14, 2016, https://www.sentencing project.org/publications/color-of-justice-racial-and-ethnic-disparity-in-state -prisons/.
4. Nellis, "Color of Justice."
5. Nellis.
6. Michelle Alexander, *The New Jim Crow* (New York: New Press, 2012), 230–231.
7. "Luzerne 'Kids for Cash' Scandal," Juvenile Law Center, n.d., https://jlc.org /luzerne-kids-cash-scandal.
8. "Luzerne 'Kids for Cash' Scandal."

Chapter 9: The Consumption of Bodies

1. Hugh Welchel, "A Biblical View of Dominion: Stewardship," Institute for Faith, Work & Economics, December 3, 2012, http://tifwe.org/a-biblical-view -of-dominion-stewardship/ and Willie James Jennings, *The Christian Imagination: Theology and the Origins of Race* (New Haven, CT: Yale University Press, 2010). The idea of Christian dominion is a supersessionist theology that claims Christ replaced Adam and Eve, to whom dominion was originally given (as Welchel states). We see evidence of this at work in the papal bulls that made up the Doctrine of Discovery. As Jennings says, "The inherent instability of creation means that all things may be altered in order to bring them to proper order toward saved existence" (29). This theology has more

recently been appropriated by far-right evangelicals during the 1980s to bolster the ideology of Christian nationalism.

2. Because nonbinary transgender people do not identify solely as either male or female, corresponding pronouns perpetuate harm and are often experienced as emotional violence. It is imperative that we love people enough to make the effort to recognize and use their preferred pronouns.

Chapter 10: Shiny Happy People

1. This story was told to me by a minister of the church who would like to remain anonymous.
2. Willie James Jennings, *The Christian Imagination: Theology and the Origins of Race* (New Haven, CT: Yale University Press, 2010), 17.
3. The first person to point out to me (and the rest of my class that day) that "charity is easy and justice is hard" was Bishop Clarence Laney Jr. of Monument of Faith Church in Durham, North Carolina.
4. Some of my friends claim not to believe this. They say it is in my nature to be disruptive and uncomfortable. I think perhaps they think too highly of me. I go where Jesus leads me, but only kicking and screaming.

Chapter 11

1. Louis P. Cain and Samuel H. Williamson, "Measuring Slavery in 2016 Dollars," MeasuringWorth, 2019, https://www.measuringworth.com/slavery .php.
2. The King Center, *The King Philosophy*. https://thekingcenter.org/king -philosophy/.